Southern Living

SUPER FAST

Southern

Southern Living®

SUPER
FAST
Southern

OXMOOR
HOUSE®

Welcome!

THERE'S NOTHING BETTER THAN coming home after a long day and settling into a from-scratch Southern meal. Wouldn't it be wonderful if you could whip together a complete dinner for your family in just 20 minutes? *Superfast Southern* **makes that dream a reality with every single recipe taking 20 minutes or less to prepare, and many taking only 15!**

Busy days call for easy solutions to getting dinner on the table—*fast!* Every tried-and-true recipe included comes with smart tips and helpful hints for speed, plus easy side dishes to complete the meal. Check out our **Top 10 Superfast Secrets** (page 10) for how to make any recipe with lightning speed.

So when you're hungry for classic Southern food, don't sacrifice flavor or variety just because you're short on time. With recipes for starters, snacks, main dishes, sides, desserts, and more, *Superfast Southern* is your any-occasion guide to making real Southern food, real fast!

Allison E Cox

Allison Cox, Editor

Look for **Instant Adds** *and* **Easy Sides** *to find clever store-bought toppings and simple sides that pump up the flavor in a snap.*

Contents

SOUPS IN A JIFFY 72

EXPRESS SANDWICHES 98

SPEEDY SKILLETS 128

131 Zucchini-Mint Pasta

132 Easy Skillet Pimiento Mac 'n' Cheese

135 Curried Shrimp with Peanuts

136 Shrimp Scampi

139 Shrimp Fried Rice

140 Fried Catfish with Pickled Peppers

143 Chicken Cutlets with Pecan Sauce

144 Easy Skillet Cordon Bleu

147 Chicken-Fried Steak

148 Turkey Tetrazzini

151 Quick-Start Bacon-Cheddar Mac 'n' Cheese

152 Pork-and-Green Bean Stir-Fry

155 Skillet Shepherd's Pie

156 Beef-and-Brussels Sprouts Stir-Fry

SIMPLE SUPPERS 158

161 Black-Eyed Pea Cakes with Heirloom Tomatoes and Slaw

162 Spicy Fish Tacos

165 Grilled Grouper with Watermelon Salsa

166 Crunchy Crab Cakes

169 Grilled Blackened Shrimp Kabobs

170 Garden Tomato Sauce over Pasta

172 Cheese Ravioli with Tomatoes and Mascarpone

174 Pan-Grilled Chicken with Fresh Plum Salsa

177 Mango Chutney-Glazed Chicken Skewers

178 Sesame Chicken and Garden Vegetables

181 Grilled Basil-and-Garlic Pork Chops

182 Pork Chops with Shallot-Cranberry Sauce

185 Supreme Beef Tostadas

186 Grilled Steak with Pineapple Salsa

189 Pepper Steak with Roasted Red Pepper Pesto

SNAPPY SIDES 190

HURRY UP, SUGAR! 222

TOP 10

SUPERFAST SECRETS

Learn how to cook with lightning speed! Follow these simple rules, and you can have supper ready in the blink of an eye, or at least faster than you ever have before.

1
START WITH A CLEAN AND TIDY KITCHEN.

Clear the clutter, take out the trash, and empty the sink. Draining pasta over a sink full of dishes is unnecessarily upping the difficulty level!

2
KEEP YOUR KITCHEN ORGANIZED.

With everything in its place, you'll know right where to find it at the moment you need it. Labeling pantry shelves, having a spice rack, using drawer dividers, and organizing the fridge will help you keep it all in order.

3
READ OVER THE ENTIRE RECIPE BEFORE SHOPPING.

A simple missing tool or spice can throw a wrench in your cooking plan, and it's simple to avoid. Make a complete list of ingredients, so you can get them all in one stop at a local grocery.

4
KEEP A WELL-STOCKED PANTRY.

When you run out of baking powder, for instance, add it to the grocery list even if you don't need it in the next couple of days. When you do need it, chances are it will be when you don't have time to run to the store!

5
WHILE YOU'RE AT IT, PREP A LITTLE EXTRA.

If you're chopping an onion, chop two. The time it takes to prep one more thing is less than the time it takes to prep two things separately. Squirrel away extra chopped ingredients in the freezer or fridge to speed up future recipes.

6
COOK FEWER TIMES THAN YOU EAT.

If it doesn't take much extra effort, make double the dressing or cook a whole bird instead of just the breast. You can use the extra later in the week, and you'll be thankful you thought ahead.

7
THERE'S OFTEN NO NEED TO THAW.

Many frozen vegetables or fruits don't need to thaw before adding them to a recipe, and you can generally just toss them into a hot skillet or pot. Great examples are sweet peas, corn, broccoli florets, bell pepper strips, and berries.

8
KNOW YOUR PRODUCE SECTION.

Many groceries have many ingredients washed, chopped, and bagged, ready to be used in recipes. If you know what's available, you can save yourself plenty of prep time.

9
SMALLER FOOD MAKES FOR QUICKER COOKING.

Chop vegetables or meat into smaller pieces or thinly slice if you want them to cook in a flash. Baked goods like cupcakes, muffins, and rolls bake faster in tiny vessels. Lean meats cook faster than marbled meats.

10
CRANK UP THE HEAT.

Don't ignore recipe instructions, but if you're cooking below the suggested heat, it will take much longer to cook through the food. Just don't walk away from the stove if you've got the heat turned up!

QUICK BITES

Shareable dips, nibbles, and snacks in a flash

Total time:
5 minutes

**KEEP LEFTOVERS IN
THE FRIDGE.**

PISTACHIO PESTO

Serve this pesto with small pita rounds or assorted vegetables such as baby carrots and bell pepper strips. Use leftover pesto as a topping for grilled chicken or fish.

 **SERVES 8**

- 1½ **cups loosely packed fresh cilantro leaves**
- ½ **cup loosely packed fresh dill weed**
- ½ **cup pistachio nuts**
- ½ **cup crumbled feta cheese (2 oz.)**
- ½ **cup olive oil**
- 5 **tsp. fresh lime juice**
- ¼ **tsp. ground red pepper**
- 1 **clove garlic**

1 In food processor, place all ingredients. Cover; process about 3 minutes, stopping occasionally to scrape down sides with rubber spatula, until smooth.

2 Use pesto immediately, cover tightly and refrigerate up to 3 days, or freeze up to 1 month (color of pesto will darken as it stands).

SOUTHERN SHRIMP BUTTER

This favorite Southern appetizer spread is simple to prepare and can be made a day ahead.

 SERVES 16

- 1 lb. uncooked medium shrimp, peeled, deveined
- 1 cup butter, softened
- 4 medium green onions, chopped (¼ cup)
- 1 Tbsp. chopped fresh dill weed
- 2 Tbsp. fresh lemon juice
- 2 tsp. red pepper sauce
- ¼ tsp. table salt
- ¼ tsp. freshly ground pepper

Garnish: fresh chives

1 In 3-qt. saucepan, heat 4 cups water to boiling. Add shrimp. Cover and return to a boil; reduce heat. Simmer uncovered 3 to 5 minutes or until shrimp are pink; drain. Cool.

2 In food processor, place shrimp. Cover; process, using quick on-and-off motions, until coarsely chopped. Add remaining ingredients except chives. Cover; process until smooth.

3 Spoon spread into serving bowl. Serve immediately, or cover and refrigerate up to 24 hours.

EASY SIDE

Toasted Baguette Slices: Slice a small baguette into ¼-inch slices and place on a baking sheet. Lightly spray with olive oil cooking spray and bake at 350° for 10 minutes or until toasted.

Total time:
20 minutes

IT'S SHRIMP BOIL IN A DIP.

Total time:
10 minutes

**STIR UP A QUICK
SUPER BOWL-READY
APPETIZER.**

RANCH-RÉMOULADE DIP

Spoon this rich and creamy rémoulade dip over burgers, seafood, or poultry, or use it to dress salads.

 SERVES 8-10

1   cup mayonnaise

¼   cup Ranch dressing

1   large dill pickle, diced (about ½ cup)

1   Tbsp. country-style Dijon mustard

1   Tbsp. dill pickle juice

1 Stir together all ingredients until blended. Cover and chill until ready to serve. Serve with assorted precut fresh vegetables. Store in refrigerator in an airtight container up to 1 week.

Note: We tested with Grey Poupon Country Dijon Mustard.

Carrots julienned into thin, uniform matchsticks that are 2 to 3 inches long and ⅛ inch wide make great dippers. Simply slice four sides of a cleaned, peeled carrot to form rectangles. Cut the carrot into ⅛-inch-long strips. Stack the strips, and cut them into 2- to 3-inch-long pieces.

LAYERED NACHO DIP

With plenty of veggies, sour cream, and cheese, this meatless appetizer is sure to please any crowd. Serve with corn chips or tortillas.

 SERVES 8-10

- 1 (16-oz.) can refried beans
- 2 tsp. taco seasoning mix
- 1 (6-oz.) container refrigerated avocado dip or 1 cup guacamole
- 1 (8-oz.) container sour cream
- 1 (4.5-oz.) can chopped black olives, drained
- 2 large tomatoes, diced
- 1 small onion, diced
- 1 (4-oz.) can chopped green chiles
- 1½ cups (6 oz.) shredded Monterey Jack cheese

1 Stir together beans and seasoning mix; spread mixture into an 11- x 7-inch baking dish. Spread avocado dip and sour cream evenly over bean mixture.

2 Sprinkle with olives and next 4 ingredients. Serve immediately, or cover and chill up to 4 hours.

Total time:
5 minutes

PREPARE IN SMALL CUPS FOR SINGLE SERVINGS.

SPICY ROASTED RED BELL PEPPER PIMIENTO CHEESE

A good box-style grater is essential for making the best pimiento cheese. It should give you a choice of hole sizes—a different size on each side. Use the smaller holes for grating hard cheeses, such as Parmesan, and the larger holes for shredding soft cheeses, such as Cheddar.

 SERVES 10-12

- 1¼ cups mayonnaise
- ½ (12-oz.) jar roasted red bell peppers, drained and chopped
- 2 tsp. finely grated onion
- 2 tsp. coarse-grained mustard
- ½ tsp. ground red pepper
- 2 (10-oz.) blocks sharp white Cheddar cheese, shredded

Freshly ground black pepper

1 Stir together mayonnaise and next 4 ingredients until well blended; stir in cheese and freshly ground black pepper to taste. Serve immediately, or store in an airtight container in refrigerator up to 4 days.

INSTANT ADD

Serve with Granny Smith apple slices or assorted crackers, or slather between two slices of bread for a simple lunch.

OLIVE TAPENADE

Use your favorite kinds of olives in this Provence-inspired appetizer. Fresh parsley, lemon juice, and herbes de Provence brighten the briny flavors of the olives.

 SERVES 13

- 1 cup pimiento-stuffed green olives
- ½ cup pitted kalamata olives
- ¼ cup chopped fresh flat-leaf parsley
- 3 Tbsp. olive oil
- 1 tsp. herbes de Provence
- 2 tsp. fresh lemon juice
- ½ tsp. freshly ground pepper
- 1 Tbsp. capers, drained

1 In food processor, place all ingredients except capers. Cover; process, using quick on-and-off motions, just until olives are coarsely chopped.

2 Spoon spread into serving bowl. Stir in capers. Serve immediately, or cover and chill up to 1 day ahead. Bring to room temperature before serving.

This spread is so wonderful served alongside crackers or bakery-style bread. Try a seeded bread or a cheese-topped variety.

Total time:
10 minutes

LET THE FOOD
PROCESSOR DO THE
CHOPPING FOR YOU.

Total time:
10 minutes

YOU CAN EVEN
USE FROZEN
CRAWFISH TAILS.

SPICY CRAWFISH SPREAD

This spread has all the Cajun flavor you love without any of the work of a crawfish boil. Serve with celery sticks!

SERVES 9

3 Tbsp. butter

¾ cup finely chopped onion

¾ cup finely chopped celery

4 cloves garlic, finely chopped

2 Tbsp. salt-free seasoning blend

½ tsp. ground red pepper

8 oz. peeled and cooked crawfish tails, chopped

1 (8-oz.) package cream cheese, softened

1 In an 8-inch skillet, melt butter over medium-high heat. Cook onion, celery, and garlic in butter 5 minutes, stirring frequently, until tender. Add seasoning blend and ground red pepper; cook and stir 30 seconds longer.

2 In medium bowl, mix vegetables and crawfish tails. Add cream cheese; stir gently to combine.

1

original recipe

RED PEPPER JELLY-BRIE BITES

 SERVES 10-12

- 2 (1.9-oz.) packages frozen mini-phyllo pastry shells, thawed (30 shells)
- 3 oz. Brie cheese, rind removed
- 8 tsp. red pepper jelly
- 3 Tbsp. chopped roasted salted almonds

1 Preheat oven to 350°. Place mini-phyllo pastry shells on a baking sheet. Cut Brie cheese into 30 very small pieces. Spoon ¼ rounded teaspoonful red pepper jelly into each shell; top with cheese. Sprinkle with almonds. Bake at 350° for 5 to 6 minutes or until cheese is melted.

Total time: 15 minutes

PARTY-READY CHEESE POPPERS WITH JUST 4 INGREDIENTS.

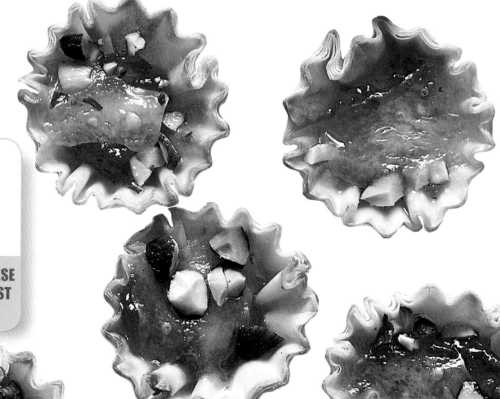

2

BLUE CHEESE + CHERRY PRESERVES =

CHERRY AND BLUE CHEESE BITES

Prepare Red Pepper Jelly-Brie Bites as directed, substituting crumbled blue cheese for Brie and cherry preserves for red pepper jelly.

3

FETA CHEESE + FIG PRESERVES + WALNUTS =

GREEK FIG BITES

Prepare Red Pepper Jelly-Brie Bites as directed, substituting crumbled feta cheese for Brie, fig preserves for red pepper jelly, and chopped toasted walnuts for almonds.

4

GOAT CHEESE + APRICOT JELLY + PECANS =

APRICOT-GOAT CHEESE BITES

Prepare Red Pepper Jelly-Brie Bites as directed, substituting crumbled goat cheese for Brie, apricot jelly for red pepper jelly, and chopped toasted pecans for almonds.

Total time:
20 minutes

SPINACH-CHEESE MIXTURE CAN BE MADE 1 DAY AHEAD.

SPINACH-AND-PARMESAN CROSTINI

Warm and cheesy, these loaded toasts pack all the flavor of creamed spinach into one crunchy bite.

SERVES 8-10

- 1 (10-oz.) package frozen spinach, thawed
- 1 (8-oz.) package cream cheese, softened
- 1 cup freshly grated Parmesan cheese
- ¼ cup mayonnaise
- 1 tsp. jarred minced garlic
- ¼ tsp. freshly ground pepper
- ½ (16-oz.) French bread loaf, cut diagonally into ½-inch-thick slices
- ⅓ cup pine nuts

1 Preheat oven to 325°. Drain spinach well, pressing between paper towels to remove excess water.

2 Stir together spinach, cream cheese, Parmesan cheese, and next 3 ingredients in a medium bowl. Top each bread slice with 2 Tbsp. cheese mixture. Sprinkle with pine nuts. Place bread slices on a baking sheet.

3 Bake at 325° for 10 minutes or until thoroughly heated and nuts are toasted.

SHRIMP SHOOTERS

Zesty with a kick of hot sauce, these fresh shrimp appetizers will add some zing to any party. Make them a day ahead.

 SERVES 8

- ⅔ cup olive oil
- ½ cup white balsamic vinegar
- 1 Tbsp. chopped fresh cilantro
- 2 Tbsp. lemon zest
- 1 tsp. table salt
- 1 tsp. freshly ground pepper
- 1 tsp. hot sauce
- 1½ lb. peeled, large cooked shrimp

Romaine lettuce leaves

1 Whisk together olive oil and next 6 ingredients in a large bowl.

2 Place cooked shrimp and vinaigrette mixture in a large zip-top plastic freezer bag. Seal and chill 24 hours, turning bag occasionally.

3 Arrange lettuce leaves in 8 (6- to 8-oz.) glasses. Spoon shrimp mixture into glasses.

Make-Ahead Note: Vinaigrette may be prepared ahead and stored in an airtight container in the refrigerator up to 1 week. Let vinaigrette come to room temperature, and whisk before adding cooked shrimp.

Total time:
15 minutes

**PREP SHRIMP AND
VINAIGRETTE THE
DAY BEFORE.**

Total time:
10 minutes

**THAW PHYLLO
SHELLS FOR
JUST 5 MINUTES.**

MINI CHICKEN SALAD BITES

Curried chicken salad is always a crowd-pleaser. Pack it in these little pastry cups, then add dried cranberries, and guests will hound you for the recipe.

 SERVES 30

- ⅓ cup mayonnaise
- 1 Tbsp. honey
- 1 tsp. curry powder
- ¼ tsp. freshly ground pepper
- ⅛ tsp. table salt
- 2 cups finely chopped cooked chicken breast
- ⅓ cup sliced almonds, toasted
- ¼ cup sweetened dried cranberries
- 2 medium green onions, chopped (2 Tbsp.)
- 2 (1.9-oz.) packages frozen mini-phyllo pastry shells, thawed (30 shells)

1 In medium bowl, mix mayonnaise, honey, curry powder, pepper, and salt. Stir in chicken, almonds, cranberries, and green onions.

2 Spoon about 1 Tbsp. chicken mixture into each shell. Serve immediately.

COUNTRY HAM MINI BISCUITS

Perfect for a special brunch or even Derby Day, these mini sandwiches are extra delicious with a drizzle of Black Pepper Honey.

 SERVES 10-12

1 (24-oz.) package frozen mini biscuits (24 biscuits)

1 (8-oz.) package thinly sliced country ham

Black Pepper Honey

1 Bake biscuits according to package directions.

2 Fill biscuits with ham. Serve with Black Pepper Honey.

Note: We tested with Mary B's Bite-Sized Buttermilk Tea Biscuits.

BLACK PEPPER HONEY

½ cup honey

2 tsp. coarsely ground pepper

2 dashes of hot sauce

1 Stir together all ingredients in a small bowl until blended.

Total time:
20 minutes

SERVE IN A BASKET
WITH HONEY
ON THE SIDE.

HORSERADISH BEEF BRUSCHETTA

The classic combination of sliced beef and horseradish spread make for the ideal appetizer topped with a sprig of watercress. If you can't find watercress, substitute arugula leaves or mesclun greens to top these beefy bites.

 **SERVES 24**

24 (¼-inch-thick) slices baguette

2 Tbsp. olive oil

¼ cup cream-style prepared horseradish

¼ cup sour cream

1 medium green onion, chopped (1 Tbsp.)

¼ lb. thinly sliced deli roast beef

½ tsp. freshly ground black pepper

½ cup watercress

1 Preheat oven to 375°. Brush both sides of bread slices with oil. Place on ungreased baking sheet. Bake at 375° for 5 minutes or until crisp. Cool 5 minutes.

2 In small bowl, mix horseradish, sour cream, and onion. Spread mixture over 1 side of each toasted bread slice. Top with beef; sprinkle with pepper. Top with watercress.

BEEF AND ASPARAGUS BUNDLES

These hearty lettuce wraps are almost a meal in one bite! To serve as a meal, this recipe makes enough for four people.

 SERVES 8

16 fresh asparagus spears

1 (4-oz.) container garlic-and-herb spreadable cheese

16 leaves Bibb lettuce (2 heads)

8 thin slices deli roast beef, cut in half

1 red bell pepper, cut into 16 strips

16 fresh chives

1 Snap off and discard tough ends of asparagus. Cut asparagus tips into 3½-inch pieces, reserving any remaining end portions for another use.

2 In a large skillet or Dutch oven, heat 2 cups lightly salted water to boiling. Add asparagus. Cover; cook 1 to 2 minutes or until crisp-tender. Remove asparagus from boiling water; immediately plunge into ice water until cold. Drain; pat dry with paper towels.

3 Spoon cheese into 1-qt. zip-top plastic freezer bag (do not seal). Cut off tiny corner of bag; squeeze bag to pipe cheese down center of each lettuce leaf. Arrange 1 roast beef slice, 1 asparagus spear, and 1 bell pepper strip in each lettuce leaf. Roll up; tie bundles with chives.

Total time:
20 minutes

**SLICE PEPPER WHILE
ASPARAGUS BOILS.**

FAST & FRESH
SALADS

Bright and happy tosses, both light and hearty

Total time:
12 minutes

SLICE GRAPES FOR A FRESH LOOK.

SPINACH-GRAPE CHOPPED SALAD

This simple salad satisfies with just a few fresh ingredients. Perfect as a light meal or side dish, or you can follow the instructions below for a heartier salad.

 SERVES 4

1 (6-oz.) package fresh baby spinach

1 cup seedless red grapes

¼ cup crumbled reduced-fat feta cheese

¼ cup bottled light raspberry-walnut vinaigrette

¼ cup toasted chopped walnuts

1 Coarsely chop spinach and grapes; toss with feta cheese and vinaigrette. Sprinkle with walnuts. Serve immediately.

Top this salad with store-bought sliced grilled chicken for a heartier meal.

CAESAR SALAD BITES

Turn these appetizers into a pretty salad by layering veggies and croutons in a clear bowl or trifle dish and topping with dressing and parsley.

 SERVES 8

- 2 romaine lettuce hearts
- ⅔ cup bottled refrigerated creamy Caesar dressing
- ½ English cucumber, chopped
- 1¼ cups small seasoned croutons
- 1 cup sliced grape tomatoes
- ¼ cup coarsely chopped fresh parsley

1 Separate romaine hearts into 24 medium leaves, and arrange on a large platter. Spoon dressing lightly down center of each leaf. Top with chopped cucumber and next 3 ingredients. Sprinkle with freshly ground pepper to taste.

Note: We tested with Marie's Creamy Caesar Dressing.

Total time:
20 minutes

**DON'T CHOP
THE ROMAINE—LEAVE
LEAVES WHOLE.**

Total time:
20 minutes

**ADD AVOCADO
AT THE
LAST MINUTE.**

BLACK BEAN SALAD

To give this salad a little more heft, serve it alongside some tortilla chips. Buy an assortment of blue and yellow tortilla chips, and toss them together for interest.

Fast & Fresh Salads

SERVES 6-8

- 3 ears fresh corn
- 3 to 4 Tbsp. lime juice
- 2 Tbsp. olive oil
- 1 Tbsp. red wine vinegar
- 1 tsp. table salt
- ½ tsp. freshly ground pepper
- 2 (15-oz.) cans black beans, drained and rinsed
- 2 large tomatoes, seeded and chopped
- 3 jalapeño peppers, seeded and chopped
- 1 small red onion, chopped
- 1 avocado, peeled, seeded, and chopped
- ¼ cup loosely packed fresh cilantro leaves

1 Cook corn in boiling water to cover 5 minutes; drain and cool. Cut kernels from cobs.

2 Whisk together lime juice and next 4 ingredients in a large bowl. Add corn, black beans, and remaining ingredients; toss to coat. Cover and chill until ready to serve.

BLUEBERRY FIELDS SALAD

Fresh blueberries, red onion, and tangy blue cheese rev up the flavor of this crisp green salad.

 SERVES 8

½   cup balsamic vinegar

⅓   cup blueberry preserves

⅓   cup olive oil

1   cup toasted chopped walnuts

2   (5.5-oz.) packages spring greens and baby spinach mix

2   cups fresh blueberries

1   small red onion, halved and sliced

1   cup crumbled blue cheese

1 Whisk together balsamic vinegar and next 2 ingredients in a small bowl. Add salt and freshly ground pepper to taste.

2 Combine walnuts, greens, and next 3 ingredients in a large bowl. Drizzle with desired amount of vinaigrette, and toss to combine. Serve immediately with remaining vinaigrette.

INSTANT ADD

Shredded rotisserie chicken is a great addition to make this a dinner salad.

Total time:
15 minutes

BUY PRESLICED ONION IN THE PRODUCE DEPARTMENT.

**Total time:
15 minutes**

USE ANY HONEY-
ROASTED NUT YOU
HAVE ON HAND.

WALDORF SPINACH SALAD

Cinnamon is the suprise ingredient in this Cheddar and apple salad with cashews and raisins.

 SERVES 6

¼ cup honey

3 Tbsp. vegetable oil

2 Tbsp. apple cider vinegar

½ tsp. dry mustard

¼ tsp. ground cinnamon

1 garlic clove, pressed

⅛ tsp. table salt

1 (9-oz.) package fresh spinach

2 large Gala apples, thinly sliced

4 oz. extra-sharp white Cheddar cheese, shaved

1 cup thinly sliced celery

1 cup honey-roasted cashews

½ cup golden raisins

1 Whisk together first 7 ingredients in a large serving bowl until well blended. Add spinach and remaining ingredients, tossing gently to coat. Serve immediately.

SPRING GREENS WITH STRAWBERRIES

Fresh dill awakens this strawberry salad while avocado adds a creamy element to balance a tangy, homemade dressing.

 SERVES 8

- ½ cup olive oil
- ¼ cup red wine vinegar
- 3 Tbsp. honey
- 1 small shallot, finely chopped
- 1 tsp. Dijon mustard
- ½ tsp. table salt
- ¼ tsp. freshly ground black pepper
- 1 (5-oz.) package arugula
- 1 (4-oz.) package watercress
- 1 pt. fresh strawberries, sliced
- ¼ cup chopped fresh dill
- 1 avocado, peeled, seeded, and cut into 1-inch pieces

1 Whisk together first 7 ingredients in a small bowl until blended. Cover and chill until ready to serve.

2 Toss together arugula and next 3 ingredients in a large bowl. Top with avocado, and drizzle with half of vinaigrette just before serving; toss. Serve with remaining vinaigrette.

Total time:
20 minutes

**BUY STEAMED FISH
AT THE GROCERY.**

GREEK SALSA SALAD WITH GROUPER

If you have 20 minutes, then you have time to make this Mediterranean salad. Pick up steamed fish from your grocery seafood counter.

SERVES 4

- 1 (8-oz.) round artisan bread loaf
- 2 Tbsp. butter, melted
- 1 tsp. minced garlic
- 1 (5-oz.) package mixed salad greens with herbs
- 1½ lb. steamed grouper fillets, broken into bite-size pieces
- 2 large tomatoes, quartered
- 1 cucumber, seeded and thinly sliced into half moons
- 1 (8-oz.) container refrigerated prechopped tri-colored bell peppers
- 1 (3-oz.) container refrigerated presliced green onions
- 1 cup refrigerated Greek vinaigrette with feta cheese and garlic

1 Preheat oven to 425°. Cut bread into 1-inch cubes (about 2 cups), and place in a single layer on a jelly-roll pan. Combine butter and garlic; drizzle over bread cubes, and toss to coat. Bake at 425° for 5 to 7 minutes or until lightly toasted, stirring twice. Transfer bread to a wire rack, and cool completely (about 5 minutes).

2 Arrange salad greens and next 5 ingredients on individual serving plates. Top with bread cubes, and serve with vinaigrette.

Note: We tested with Marie's Greek Vinaigrette with Feta Cheese & Garlic.

SPRING SALMON AND VEGETABLE SALAD

Line your pan with foil for easy cleanup with the broiled salmon. This dressing will keep in the fridge up to one week.

SERVES 4-6

- ½ lb. fresh asparagus
- 1 cup sugar snap peas
- 1¼ lb. skinless salmon fillets, cut into 2-inch chunks
- ½ tsp. table salt
- ¼ tsp. black pepper
- 6 cups chopped romaine lettuce hearts
- ½ cup uncooked shelled fresh or frozen edamame, thawed
- ¼ cup sliced radishes

Creamy Herb Dressing

1 Preheat broiler with oven rack 6 inches from heat. Snap off tough ends of asparagus. Cut asparagus into 1-inch-long pieces, and cook with sugar snap peas in boiling salted water 2 to 3 minutes or until crisp-tender; drain. Plunge into ice water; drain.

2 Sprinkle salmon with salt and pepper; broil on a lightly greased rack in a broiler pan 3 to 4 minutes or to desired degree of doneness.

3 Arrange lettuce, edamame, radishes, asparagus mixture, and salmon on a serving plate. Drizzle with dressing.

CREAMY HERB DRESSING

- ½ cup buttermilk
- ¼ cup mayonnaise
- 3 Tbsp. chopped fresh herbs (such as mint, dill, and chives)
- 1 Tbsp. fresh lemon juice

1 Whisk together buttermilk, mayonnaise, chopped fresh herbs, fresh lemon juice, and salt and pepper to taste. Chill 30 minutes.

Total time:
20 minutes

BUY PRECHOPPED
AND WASHED
ROMAINE LETTUCE.

Total time:
15 minutes

ROLL SMOKED SALMON PIECES FOR A PRETTY PRESENTATION.

SALMON SALAD WITH AVOCADO

Packaged smoked salmon and prepackaged arugula make this dinner come together in just 15 minutes.

 SERVES 6-8

¼ cup olive oil

3 Tbsp. fresh lemon juice

1 tsp. Dijon mustard

¾ tsp. sugar

½ tsp. kosher salt

¼ tsp. freshly ground black pepper

1 (5-oz.) package arugula*

6 radishes, thinly sliced

2 (4-oz.) packages thinly sliced smoked salmon

1 avocado, peeled, seeded and sliced

1 Whisk together first 6 ingredients. Gently toss together arugula, radishes, and half of olive oil mixture in a large bowl. Arrange on a serving platter with salmon and avocado. Serve immediately with remaining olive oil mixture.

*1 (5-oz.) package spring mix may be substituted.

1

original recipe

CHEF'S SALAD

 SERVES 6

- 8 cups mixed salad greens
- 2 cups chopped mixed fresh vegetables
- ½ small red onion, cut in half and thinly sliced
- 3 cups coarsely chopped cooked chicken
- 1 large avocado, peeled, seeded, and sliced
- 6 cooked bacon slices, crumbled
- 3 cups large-cut croutons

Bottled refrigerated Ranch dressing

1 Toss together first 3 ingredients. Top with chicken and avocado; sprinkle with bacon and croutons. Serve with dressing.

Total time:
10 minutes

MIX UP THE FLAVORS AND MAKE SALADS ENTICING.

2

YELLOW BELL PEPPERS + MUSHROOMS + RADISHES =

SPRING GARDEN
CHEF SALAD

Prepare Chef's Salad as directed, using sliced yellow peppers, chopped mushrooms, and sliced radishes for the vegetables. Serve with bottled raspberry vinaigrette instead of Ranch dressing.

3

GRAPES + ALMONDS =

WALDORF
CHEF SALAD

Prepare Chef's Salad as directed, substituting sliced grapes for the avocado and ¾ cup sliced almonds for the croutons. Serve with bottled creamy poppy seed dressing instead of Ranch.

4

CURRY + PEANUTS =

THAI CURRY
CHEF SALAD

Prepare Chef's Salad as directed, using shredded carrots and chopped cucumbers for the vegetables and substituting ¾ cup chopped peanuts for the croutons. Serve with bottled curry yogurt dressing instead of Ranch dressing.

Total time:
20 minutes

SO EASY TO JUST TOSS AND SERVE!

GREEK CHICKEN SALAD

Fresh parsley and mint are essential to create that fresh Greek flavor that is so popular. Don't be tempted to use dried herbs!

 SERVES 8

2	heads romaine lettuce, torn
2	medium tomatoes, chopped
1	large cucumber, chopped
¼	cup chopped fresh parsley
¼	cup chopped green onions
1	tsp. chopped fresh mint
3	cups chopped cooked chicken
4	oz. crumbled feta cheese
½	cup pitted kalamata or black olives, coarsely chopped
1	cup bottled Greek salad dressing

1 Combine first 6 ingredients in a large bowl, tossing gently; top with chicken and next 2 ingredients. Drizzle with desired amount of Greek salad dressing.

CHICKEN BLT SALAD

This tempting chicken salad is a play on the classic BLT. Choose center-cut bacon, which is lower in fat and has 20 percent fewer calories.

Fast & Fresh Salads

 SERVES 4

- ½ cup buttery garlic-and-herb spreadable cheese
- 3 cups chopped cooked chicken (about 6 breast halves)
- ½ cup grape tomatoes, halved
- ⅓ cup chopped green onion tops
- 2 bacon slices, cooked and crumbled
- 1/16 tsp. table salt
- ⅛ tsp. freshly ground black pepper

Assorted mixed greens (optional)

1 Microwave cheese in a small microwave-safe bowl at HIGH 20 seconds. Stir in next 4 ingredients, tossing well. Add salt and pepper. Serve on assorted greens, if desired.

Note: We tested with Alouette Garlic & Herbs Spreadable Cheese.

Total time:
15 minutes

**SERVE PROSCIUTTO
PIECES WHOLE
OR CRUMBLED.**

MELON AND CRISPY PROSCIUTTO SALAD

Use any melon to build the base of this sweet, salty, and crunchy salad.

 SERVES 4

- 1 (4-oz.) package prosciutto
- 6 Tbsp. chopped fresh mint
- 4 Tbsp. olive oil
- 3 Tbsp. white wine vinegar
- 3 Tbsp. honey
- ¾ tsp. kosher salt
- ½ tsp. freshly ground pepper
- 10 cups loosely packed baby greens (such as arugula)
- ½ honeydew melon, peeled, seeded, and coarsely chopped (about 6 cups)
- 1 (4-oz.) package feta cheese, crumbled
- ½ cup pistachios, coarsely chopped

1 Arrange half of prosciutto on a paper towel-lined microwave-safe plate; cover with a paper towel. Microwave at HIGH 2 minutes or until crisp. Repeat procedure with remaining prosciutto. Break prosciutto into large pieces.

2 Whisk together mint and next 5 ingredients.

3 Toss greens and chopped melon with vinaigrette, and top with cooked prosciutto, crumbled feta cheese, and chopped pistachios.

TEX-MEX BEEF-AND-BEANS CHOPPED SALAD

Expect lots of crunch and flavor in this kicking salad, thanks to tortilla chips, pepper Jack cheese, cucumber, and jicama.

 SERVES 6

- ¾ cup bottled Ranch dressing
- ¾ cup refrigerated salsa
- 2 (10-oz.) packages romaine lettuce hearts, chopped
- 1 (15-oz.) can black beans, drained and rinsed
- 3 cups coarsely crushed tortilla chips
- 6 oz. pepper Jack cheese, cut into small cubes
- 1 cup seeded and chopped cucumber
- 1 cup diced jicama
- 3 plum tomatoes, chopped
- 1 medium avocado, chopped
- ¾ lb. sliced barbecued beef brisket (without sauce), warmed

1 Stir together first 2 ingredients in a small bowl.

2 Toss together romaine and next 7 ingredients. Drizzle with dressing mixture, and top with brisket. Serve immediately.

Total time:
20 minutes

**FIND REFRIGERATED
SALSA IN THE
DELI SECTION.**

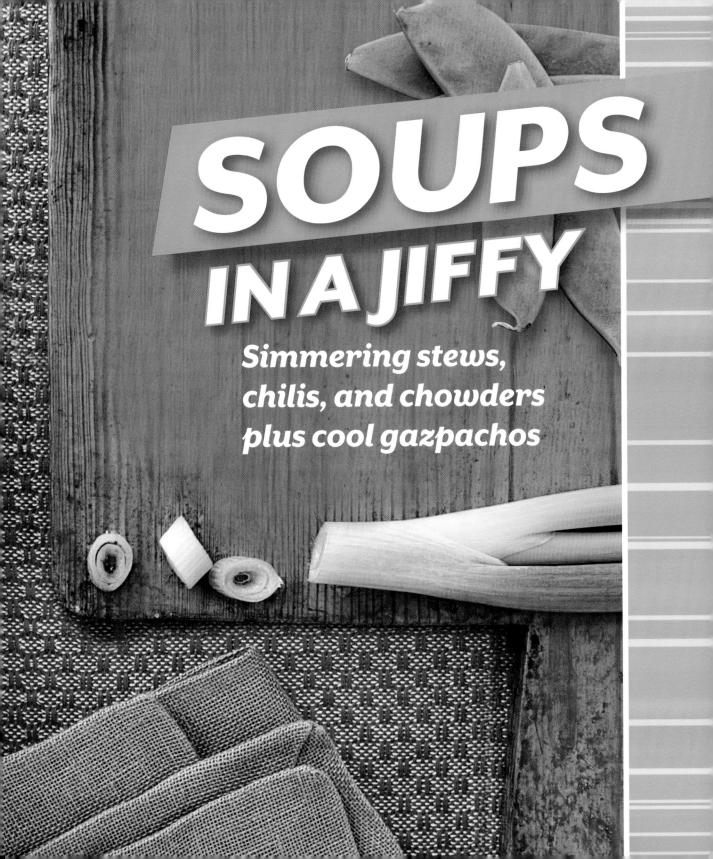

SOUPS
IN A JIFFY

*Simmering stews,
chilis, and chowders
plus cool gazpachos*

Total time:
18 minutes

THIS VEGETARIAN
CHILI COOKS
UP FAST.

MEATLESS CHILI

This chili also works as a burrito filling. Just spoon some chili onto a warm flour tortilla, sprinkle with shredded lettuce and cheese, and roll up.

 **SERVES 4**

Cooking spray

2   tsp. jarred minced garlic

1   large onion, chopped

1   (16-oz.) can chili-hot
    beans, undrained

1   (14.5-oz.) can no-salt-
    added diced tomatoes,
    undrained

1   tsp. chili powder

1   tsp. ground cumin

12 oz. frozen vegetable and
    grain protein crumbles
    (about 3 cups)

1 Coat a 4-qt. saucepan with cooking spray. Place pan over medium-high heat. Add garlic and onion; sauté 3 minutes. Add beans and next 3 ingredients. Bring to a boil, stirring occasionally; reduce heat, and simmer 5 minutes. Add protein crumbles, and cook 3 minutes or until thoroughly heated.

SWEET POTATO SOUP

Ground red pepper adds a spicy kick to this soup. You can prepare and chill the soup a day or two ahead, if you'd like. Just reheat it in the microwave, in a slow cooker, or on the cooktop.

Soups in a Jiffy

SERVES 8

- 1 (40-oz.) can yams in heavy syrup
- 1 (14-oz.) can vegetable or chicken broth
- ½ cup fresh orange juice
- 1 to 2 Tbsp. minced fresh ginger
- 1½ cups coconut milk
- 1 tsp. table salt
- ¼ tsp. ground red pepper (optional)

Garnishes: coconut milk, fresh thyme sprig

1. Drain yams, reserving ½ cup syrup. Discard remaining syrup. Place yams in a blender or food processor. Add ½ cup syrup, broth, orange juice, and ginger. Process 2 to 3 minutes or until smooth, stopping to scrape down sides.

2. Pour pureed mixture into a medium saucepan. Stir in coconut milk, salt, and red pepper, if desired. Cook over medium heat, stirring often, until soup is thoroughly heated. Ladle soup into bowls.

Note: We tested with A Taste of Thai Coconut Milk.

Total time:
15 minutes

CANNED YAMS SPEED UP THIS SOUP.

Total time:
15 minutes

BLOODY MARY MIX ADDS FLAVOR AND EASE TO THIS SOUP.

INSTANT GAZPACHO

The perfect summer soup, this version is left chunky with all the diced vegetables. If you want a smoother soup, you can process it in the blender.

SERVES 4

- 5   green onions, sliced
- 1   small red bell pepper, diced
- 1   small cucumber, diced
- 2   plum tomatoes, diced
- 3   cups Bloody Mary mix
- ¼   tsp. table salt
- ¼   tsp. pepper

1 Stir together all ingredients. Cover and chill until ready to serve. Ladle soup into bowls.

Soups in a Jiffy

INSTANT ADD

A dollop of sour cream or crème fraîche puts this chilled soup over the top by balancing out the crisp veggies.

1

original recipe

TOMATO-BASIL BISQUE

🍲 **SERVES 6 TO 8**

- 2 (10¾-oz.) cans tomato soup
- 1 (14½-oz.) can diced tomatoes
- 2½ cups buttermilk
- 2 Tbsp. chopped fresh basil
- ¼ tsp. freshly ground black pepper

Toppings: fresh basil leaves, freshly ground black pepper, shaved Parmesan cheese

1 Cook first 5 ingredients in a 3-qt. saucepan over medium heat, stirring often, 6 to 8 minutes or until thoroughly heated. Serve immediately with desired toppings.

Total time: 15 minutes

CANNED SOUP AND TOMATOES MAKE IT SNAPPY!

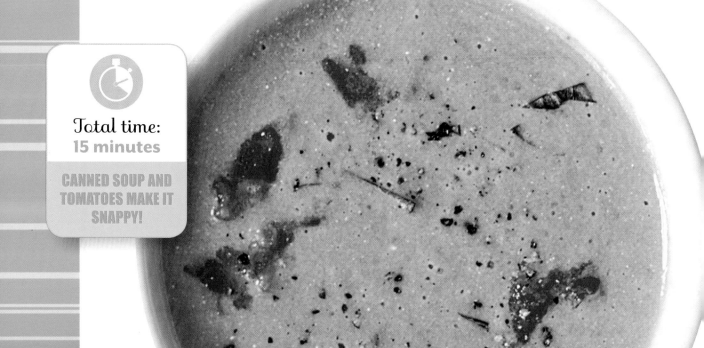

GREEK CHICKEN SALAD

Fresh parsley and mint are essential to create that fresh Greek flavor that is so popular. Don't be tempted to use dried herbs!

 SERVES 8

- 2 heads romaine lettuce, torn
- 2 medium tomatoes, chopped
- 1 large cucumber, chopped
- ¼ cup chopped fresh parsley
- ¼ cup chopped green onions
- 1 tsp. chopped fresh mint
- 3 cups chopped cooked chicken
- 4 oz. crumbled feta cheese
- ½ cup pitted kalamata or black olives, coarsely chopped
- 1 cup bottled Greek salad dressing

1 Combine first 6 ingredients in a large bowl, tossing gently; top with chicken and next 2 ingredients. Drizzle with desired amount of Greek salad dressing.

CHICKEN BLT SALAD

This tempting chicken salad is a play on the classic BLT. Choose center-cut bacon, which is lower in fat and has 20 percent fewer calories.

 SERVES 4

½ cup buttery garlic-and-herb spreadable cheese

3 cups chopped cooked chicken (about 6 breast halves)

½ cup grape tomatoes, halved

⅓ cup chopped green onion tops

2 bacon slices, cooked and crumbled

¹⁄₁₆ tsp. table salt

⅛ tsp. freshly ground black pepper

Assorted mixed greens (optional)

1 Microwave cheese in a small microwave-safe bowl at HIGH 20 seconds. Stir in next 4 ingredients, tossing well. Add salt and pepper. Serve on assorted greens, if desired.

Note: We tested with Alouette Garlic & Herbs Spreadable Cheese.

Total time:
15 minutes

ROTISSERIE CHICKEN MAKES THIS EASY AND QUICK.

Total time:
15 minutes

SERVE PROSCIUTTO PIECES WHOLE OR CRUMBLED.

MELON AND CRISPY PROSCIUTTO SALAD

Use any melon to build the base of this sweet, salty, and crunchy salad.

SERVES 4

- 1 (4-oz.) package prosciutto
- 6 Tbsp. chopped fresh mint
- 4 Tbsp. olive oil
- 3 Tbsp. white wine vinegar
- 3 Tbsp. honey
- ¾ tsp. kosher salt
- ½ tsp. freshly ground pepper
- 10 cups loosely packed baby greens (such as arugula)
- ½ honeydew melon, peeled, seeded, and coarsely chopped (about 6 cups)
- 1 (4-oz.) package feta cheese, crumbled
- ½ cup pistachios, coarsely chopped

1 Arrange half of prosciutto on a paper towel-lined microwave-safe plate; cover with a paper towel. Microwave at HIGH 2 minutes or until crisp. Repeat procedure with remaining prosciutto. Break prosciutto into large pieces.

2 Whisk together mint and next 5 ingredients.

3 Toss greens and chopped melon with vinaigrette, and top with cooked prosciutto, crumbled feta cheese, and chopped pistachios.

TEX-MEX BEEF-AND-BEANS CHOPPED SALAD

Expect lots of crunch and flavor in this kicking salad, thanks to tortilla chips, pepper Jack cheese, cucumber, and jicama.

Fast & Fresh Salads

SERVES 6

- ¾ cup bottled Ranch dressing
- ¾ cup refrigerated salsa
- 2 (10-oz.) packages romaine lettuce hearts, chopped
- 1 (15-oz.) can black beans, drained and rinsed
- 3 cups coarsely crushed tortilla chips
- 6 oz. pepper Jack cheese, cut into small cubes
- 1 cup seeded and chopped cucumber
- 1 cup diced jicama
- 3 plum tomatoes, chopped
- 1 medium avocado, chopped
- ¾ lb. sliced barbecued beef brisket (without sauce), warmed

1 Stir together first 2 ingredients in a small bowl.

2 Toss together romaine and next 7 ingredients. Drizzle with dressing mixture, and top with brisket. Serve immediately.

Total time:
20 minutes

FIND REFRIGERATED SALSA IN THE DELI SECTION.

SOUPS
IN A JIFFY

*Simmering stews,
chilis, and chowders
plus cool gazpachos*

Total time:
18 minutes

THIS VEGETARIAN
CHILI COOKS
UP FAST.

MEATLESS CHILI

This chili also works as a burrito filling. Just spoon some chili onto a warm flour tortilla, sprinkle with shredded lettuce and cheese, and roll up.

 **SERVES 4**

Cooking spray

2   tsp. jarred minced garlic

1   large onion, chopped

1   (16-oz.) can chili-hot beans, undrained

1   (14.5-oz.) can no-salt-added diced tomatoes, undrained

1   tsp. chili powder

1   tsp. ground cumin

12 oz. frozen vegetable and grain protein crumbles (about 3 cups)

1 Coat a 4-qt. saucepan with cooking spray. Place pan over medium-high heat. Add garlic and onion; sauté 3 minutes. Add beans and next 3 ingredients. Bring to a boil, stirring occasionally; reduce heat, and simmer 5 minutes. Add protein crumbles, and cook 3 minutes or until thoroughly heated.

SWEET POTATO SOUP

Ground red pepper adds a spicy kick to this soup. You can prepare and chill the soup a day or two ahead, if you'd like. Just reheat it in the microwave, in a slow cooker, or on the cooktop.

Soups in a Jiffy

SERVES 8

- 1 (40-oz.) can yams in heavy syrup
- 1 (14-oz.) can vegetable or chicken broth
- ½ cup fresh orange juice
- 1 to 2 Tbsp. minced fresh ginger
- 1½ cups coconut milk
- 1 tsp. table salt
- ¼ tsp. ground red pepper (optional)

Garnishes: **coconut milk, fresh thyme sprig**

1. Drain yams, reserving ½ cup syrup. Discard remaining syrup. Place yams in a blender or food processor. Add ½ cup syrup, broth, orange juice, and ginger. Process 2 to 3 minutes or until smooth, stopping to scrape down sides.

2. Pour pureed mixture into a medium saucepan. Stir in coconut milk, salt, and red pepper, if desired. Cook over medium heat, stirring often, until soup is thoroughly heated. Ladle soup into bowls.

Note: We tested with A Taste of Thai Coconut Milk.

Total time:
15 minutes

CANNED YAMS SPEED
UP THIS SOUP.

Total time:
15 minutes

BLOODY MARY MIX ADDS FLAVOR AND EASE TO THIS SOUP.

INSTANT GAZPACHO

The perfect summer soup, this version is left chunky with all the diced vegetables. If you want a smoother soup, you can process it in the blender.

SERVES 4

- 5 green onions, sliced
- 1 small red bell pepper, diced
- 1 small cucumber, diced
- 2 plum tomatoes, diced
- 3 cups Bloody Mary mix
- ¼ tsp. table salt
- ¼ tsp. pepper

1 Stir together all ingredients. Cover and chill until ready to serve. Ladle soup into bowls.

INSTANT ADD

A dollop of sour cream or crème fraîche puts this chilled soup over the top by balancing out the crisp veggies.

1

original recipe
TOMATO-BASIL BISQUE

SERVES 6 TO 8

- 2 (10¾-oz.) cans tomato soup
- 1 (14½-oz.) can diced tomatoes
- 2½ cups buttermilk
- 2 Tbsp. chopped fresh basil
- ¼ tsp. freshly ground black pepper
- *Toppings*: fresh basil leaves, freshly ground black pepper, shaved Parmesan cheese

1 Cook first 5 ingredients in a 3-qt. saucepan over medium heat, stirring often, 6 to 8 minutes or until thoroughly heated. Serve immediately with desired toppings.

Total time: 15 minutes

CANNED SOUP AND TOMATOES MAKE IT SNAPPY!

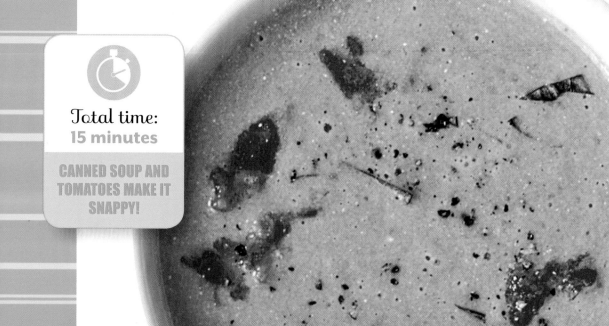

2

FIRE-ROASTED TOMATOES + GREEN CHILES =
FIERY
TOMATO BISQUE

Prepare Tomato-Basil Bisque as directed,
omitting basil. Substitute fire-roasted
diced tomatoes for diced tomatoes and
stir in 1 (4-oz.) can chopped green
chiles, undrained, along with
tomatoes. Serve with tortilla chips.

3

FONTINA CHEESE =
CHEESY
TOMATO BISQUE

Prepare Tomato-Basil Bisque as directed.
Ladle soup into 6 ovenproof crocks and
top each serving with 2 Tbsp. grated
Fontina cheese. Place crocks on a baking sheet
and place under broiler for 1 minute or until
cheese melts. Serve with baguette slices.

4

CILANTRO + RED CURRY PASTE =
CURRIED
TOMATO BISQUE

Prepare Tomato-Basil Bisque as directed,
substituting chopped fresh cilantro for basil.
Whisk in 2 tsp. red curry paste. Garnish
with cilantro leaves. Serve with
store-bought naan bread.

Total time:
20 minutes

PRESHREDDED
CARROTS SAVE
PREP TIME.

WHITE BEAN SOUP

Ham gives this soup a punch of flavor. Using canned ham and beans keeps things simple.

Soups in a Jiffy

SERVES 3

- 1 (16-oz.) can navy beans, undrained
- 1 (15.8-oz.) can great Northern beans, undrained
- ¼ cup chopped onion
- ½ cup preshredded carrot
- ¼ cup butter, melted
- 1 (5-oz.) can chunk ham, drained and flaked

1 Combine beans in a large saucepan; mash slightly with a potato masher. Stir in 1 cup water, and cook over low heat until thoroughly heated.

2 Meanwhile, sauté onion and carrot in butter over medium-high heat until onion is tender. Add sautéed vegetables and ham to bean mixture. Cook over low heat 10 minutes, stirring occasionally.

PEPPER GAZPACHO

Soups in a Jiffy

SERVES 8

1 (46-oz.) bottle vegetable juice

1 (12-oz.) jar roasted red bell peppers, drained

1 cup loosely packed fresh parsley leaves

½ cup chopped fresh basil leaves

1 cup chopped cucumber

½ cup banana pepper rings

2 garlic cloves

3 Tbsp. fresh lemon juice

2 Tbsp. extra virgin olive oil

Garnishes: sliced cucumber, fresh basil sprig

1 Process half of vegetable juice and next 7 ingredients in a blender until smooth. Transfer to a large bowl. Stir in remaining vegetable juice and 2 Tbsp. olive oil. Serve immediately, or cover and chill up to 2 days.

EASY SIDE

Greek Salad Focaccia: Combine 2½ cups mixed salad greens, ½ cup sliced red onion, 3 Tbsp. crumbled feta cheese, 1 Tbsp. lemon juice, 1 Tbsp. olive oil, and ⅛ tsp. crushed red pepper in a bowl, tossing well to coat. Cut 1 (6-oz.) focaccia bread in half horizontally. Arrange salad on bottom half. Replace top half of loaf; cut into equal portions.

Total time:
10 minutes

A BOTTLE OF
VEGETABLE JUICE
STARTS IT OFF QUICK.

Total time:
20 minutes

PREPARE NOODLES
AND REST OF SOUP AT
THE SAME TIME.

SPICY SHRIMP NOODLE BOWL

This recipe is made super-quick by using a package of flavored noodles. Add in some shrimp, fresh vegetables, and broth, and you've got a great meal in no time.

SERVES 4

- 1 (8.2-oz.) package soy-ginger-flavored Asian-style noodles
- 2 (14.5-oz.) cans chicken broth
- 1 lb. peeled and deveined medium-size raw shrimp (31-40 count)
- ¼ cup spicy Szechuan sauce
- 2 cups shredded napa cabbage
- 1 cup fresh snow peas, trimmed and cut into 1-inch pieces
- ¾ cup matchstick carrots
- ¼ cup loosely packed fresh cilantro leaves
- 3 green onions, thinly sliced

1 Cook noodles according to package directions, omitting flavor packet; drain.

2 Stir together flavor packet from noodles and chicken broth in a 3-qt. saucepan. Bring to a boil; add shrimp, and cook 3 minutes. Stir in Szechuan sauce and next 3 ingredients. Cook 2 minutes. Stir in noodles, cilantro, and green onions.

Note: We tested with Annie Chun's All Natural Asian Cuisine Soy Ginger Meal Starter and House of Tsang Szechuan Spicy Stir Fry Sauce.

SO-QUICK SEAFOOD CHOWDER

Frozen tilapia fillets are great to keep on hand for weeknight dinners.

SERVES 6

12 oz. fresh or frozen orange roughy fillets, thawed

½ (24-oz.) package frozen hash browns with onions and peppers

1 (12-oz.) can evaporated milk

1 (10¾-oz.) can cream of potato soup, undiluted

¼ cup bacon bits

2 tsp. chopped fresh dill or ¾ tsp. dried dill weed

¼ tsp. table salt

¼ tsp. pepper

1 (2-oz.) jar diced pimientos, drained

Garnish: chopped fresh dill

1 Cut fish fillets into 1-inch pieces.

2 Bring hash browns to a boil in 1 cup water in a large saucepan; reduce heat to low, cover, and simmer 5 minutes or until tender.

3 Stir in evaporated milk and next 5 ingredients; return to a boil. Add fish and pimientos; cover, reduce heat, and simmer 3 to 5 minutes or until fish flakes easily. Serve immediately.

Note: We tested with Ore-Ida Potatoes O'Brien and Hormel Real Bacon Bits.

Total time:
20 minutes

THAW FROZEN
FILLETS IN
COLD WATER.

Total time:
20 minutes

SERVE WITH ANY
CRACKERS YOU HAVE
ON HAND.

CRAB AND OYSTER BISQUE

Fresh shucked oysters are the star in this chowder-like soup. Look for oysters that are damp, uniform in size, fresh-smelling, and packaged in clear oyster liquor.

SERVES 10

- ¼ cup butter
- 4 cloves garlic, finely chopped
- 2 shallots, finely chopped
- 3 Tbsp. all-purpose flour
- 1 (8-oz.) bottle clam juice
- 1 cup dry white wine
- 1 Tbsp. Worcestershire sauce
- 1 tsp. Cajun seasoning
- ¼ tsp. pepper
- 4 cups whipping cream
- 1 (12-oz.) container fresh oysters, drained
- 1 lb. fresh lump crabmeat

Garnish: chopped fresh flat-leaf parsley

1 In a 4- to 5-qt. Dutch oven, melt butter over medium heat. Cook garlic and shallots in butter, stirring occasionally, until tender. Add flour; cook 1 minute, stirring constantly. Add clam juice and wine; cook 2 minutes, stirring constantly, until thickened.

2 Stir in Worcestershire sauce, Cajun seasoning, pepper, and whipping cream. Cook until thoroughly heated, about 10 minutes. Stir in oysters and crabmeat; cook just until edges of oysters curl.

ITALIAN GNOCCHI SOUP

This soup is a hearty meatless dinner option for your family. For a meaty version, add crumbled cooked Italian sausage.

Soups in a Jiffy

🍲 **SERVES 8**

- 1 (32-oz.) carton vegetable broth
- 1 (14.5-oz.) can diced tomatoes with basil, garlic, and oregano, undrained
- 1 (16-oz.) package gnocchi (not refrigerated or frozen)
- 1 (6-oz.) package fresh baby spinach leaves
- ½ tsp. freshly ground pepper
- ½ cup basil pesto
- ½ cup freshly grated Parmesan cheese

1 In 4-qt. Dutch oven, bring broth and tomatoes to a boil. Add gnocchi. Return to a boil; reduce heat. Simmer 2 to 4 minutes or until gnocchi float to top.

2 Gradually add spinach, stirring until wilted. Stir in pepper.

3 Ladle into bowls, and top each serving with 1 Tbsp. pesto and 1 Tbsp. cheese.

Total time:
15 minutes

LOOK FOR DRIED GNOCCHI IN THE PASTA AISLE.

Total time:
20 minutes

USE GROUND
ROUND—NOT
SIRLOIN OR CHUCK.

EASY TEXAS CHILI

Chili-hot beans and a 15-minute simmer to blend flavors make this the fastest chili around.

SERVES 4

- 1 lb. ground round
- 1 cup chopped onion
- 1 tsp. jarred minced garlic
- 1 (16-oz.) can chili-hot beans, drained
- 1 (6-oz.) can tomato paste
- 1 Tbsp. chili powder

1 Combine first 3 ingredients in a Dutch oven; cook until beef is browned, stirring until it crumbles. Add beans, tomato paste, 1½ cups water, and chili powder; cover, reduce heat, and simmer 15 minutes, stirring occasionally.

INSTANT ADD

Store-bought cornbread is the best and easiest accompaniment to chili. Just cover in foil and warm in a 350° oven.

BEEFY MINESTRONE SOUP

This classic Italian soup combines lots of veggies with pasta and beef. Who knew you could use deli roast beef in a soup?

Soups
in a Jiffy

SERVES 6

- ⅔ cup uncooked ditalini (very short, tube-shaped macaroni)
- 2 (14-oz.) cans lower-sodium fat-free beef broth
- 1 (14.5-oz.) can no-salt-added stewed tomatoes, undrained
- 2 small zucchini
- 1 (15.5-oz.) can cannellini beans or other white beans, drained and rinsed
- 2 tsp. dried Italian seasoning
- 8 oz. deli rare roast beef, sliced ¼ inch thick and diced

1. Combine first 3 ingredients in a large saucepan; cover and bring to a boil over high heat.

2. Cut zucchini in half lengthwise, and slice. Add zucchini, beans, and Italian seasoning to pasta mixture; cover, reduce heat, and simmer 6 minutes. Add beef, and cook 4 minutes or until pasta is tender.

Total time:
13 minutes

MACARONI WORKS
GREAT, TOO!

EXPRESS SANDWICHES

Deli-style stacks, subs, and wraps, plus pitas, paninis, and tacos

Total time:
20 minutes

**PREPARE CUCUMBER
SAUCE WHILE
BURGERS GRILL.**

GREEK TURKEY BURGERS

Mediterranean-inspired toppings like the Greek yogurt spread, tomatoes, and cucumber really pump up the flavor in these burgers. To make cucumber ribbons, use a Y-shaped vegetable peeler to cut thin slices of cucumber lengthwise.

SERVES 4

1⅓ lb. ground turkey breast

1 (4-oz.) package crumbled feta cheese

¼ cup finely chopped red onion

1 tsp. dried oregano

1 tsp. lemon zest

½ tsp. table salt

Vegetable cooking spray

½ cup grated English cucumber

1 (6-oz.) container fat-free Greek yogurt

1 Tbsp. chopped fresh mint

½ tsp. table salt

4 French hamburger buns, split and toasted

Toppings: lettuce leaves, tomato slices, thinly sliced cucumber

Garnish: pepperoncini salad peppers

1 Stir together first 6 ingredients. Shape mixture into 4 (½-inch-thick) patties.

2 Heat a grill pan over medium-high heat. Coat grill pan with cooking spray. Add patties; cook 5 minutes on each side or until done.

3 Stir together cucumber, yogurt, mint, and ½ tsp. salt in a small bowl. Serve burgers on buns with cucumber sauce and desired toppings.

Express Sandwiches

GOUDA CHICKEN SANDWICHES

These hoagies combine the flavors of Gouda cheese, mustard, and roasted bell peppers for a vibrant take on the chicken sandwich.

Express Sandwiches

SERVES 4

- 4   hoagie rolls
- ¼   cup mustard-mayonnaise blend
- 12   (1-oz.) Gouda cheese slices
- 3   cups cooked chicken, sliced
- 1   (7-oz.) jar roasted red bell peppers, drained and thinly sliced
- 4   green leaf lettuce leaves
- 8   tomato slices

1 Split rolls in half horizontally; spread with mustard-mayonnaise blend. Top each roll bottom with 3 cheese slices, desired amount of chicken, and roasted red pepper slices. Layer each roll top with 1 lettuce leaf and 2 tomato slices. Join top and bottom halves of rolls. Serve immediately.

EASY SIDE

Watermelon Agua Fresca: Process 4 cups seeded watermelon cubes, ⅓ cup apple juice, 2 Tbsp. fresh lime juice, 1 tsp. chopped fresh mint, ¼ to ½ tsp. ground ginger, and, if desired, 1 Tbsp. honey in a blender or food processor until smooth, stopping to scrape down sides. Cover and chill 1 hour. Pour into 4 glasses. Garnish with lime wedges and fresh mint sprigs.

Total time:
18 minutes

MAKE IT QUICK;
USE 1 (2½-LB.)
ROTISSERIE CHICKEN.

GREEK CHICKEN SALAD SANDWICH

This lighter take on chicken salad is packed with intense flavor thanks to feta, red onion, cucumber, and hummus. Try either spicy three-pepper or artichoke-and-garlic hummus for this sandwich.

SERVES 4

- 2 cups sliced romaine lettuce
- 1 cup chopped roasted chicken breast
- ⅔ cup diced seeded cucumber
- ¼ cup thinly sliced red onion
- ¼ cup (1 oz.) crumbled feta cheese
- 2 Tbsp. fresh lemon juice
- 2 Tbsp. olive oil
- ¼ tsp. table salt
- ¼ tsp. freshly ground black pepper
- 6 Tbsp. roasted red bell pepper hummus
- 2 (6-inch) whole wheat pitas, cut in half

1 Combine lettuce and next 4 ingredients in a large bowl. Add lemon juice, olive oil, salt, and pepper; toss gently.

2 Spread 1½ Tbsp. hummus inside each pita half; spoon salad mixture evenly into halves. Serve immediately.

Express Sandwiches

BLT BENEDICT WITH AVOCADO-TOMATO RELISH

This egg-centered, open-faced sandwich is perfect for lunch or even dinner. Sunny-side up or sliced boiled eggs would work just as well as poached eggs for this dish.

Express Sandwiches

SERVES 6

- 1 cup halved grape tomatoes
- 1 avocado, diced
- 1 Tbsp. chopped fresh basil
- 1 garlic clove, minced
- 2 Tbsp. extra virgin olive oil
- 1 Tbsp. red wine vinegar, divided
- 6 large eggs
- ¼ cup mayonnaise
- 6 (¾-inch-thick) bakery bread slices, toasted
- 3 cups firmly packed arugula
- 12 thick bacon slices, cooked

1. Combine tomatoes, next 4 ingredients, and 2½ tsp. red wine vinegar in a small bowl.

2. Add water to depth of 3 inches in a large saucepan. Bring to a boil; reduce heat, and maintain at a light simmer. Add remaining ½ tsp. red wine vinegar. Break eggs, and slip into water, 1 at a time, as close as possible to surface. Simmer 3 to 5 minutes or to desired degree of doneness. Remove with a slotted spoon. Trim edges, if desired.

3. Spread mayonnaise on 1 side of each bread slice. Layer each with ½ cup arugula, 2 bacon slices, and 1 egg. Top with tomato mixture. Add salt and freshly ground black pepper to taste.

Total time:
20 minutes

**CHOOSE A
HEARTY BREAD THAT
WILL HOLD UP.**

HAM-AND-FONTINA SOURDOUGH SANDWICHES

It's what's inside that counts here. Deli ham gets dressed up with good stuff like a pesto-mayonnaise spread, fontina cheese, and basil leaves.

 **SERVES 4**

- ½ cup mayonnaise
- 3 Tbsp. jarred refrigerated pesto sauce
- 1 tsp. fresh lemon juice
- 8 sourdough bakery bread slices
- 16 fontina cheese slices (about ½ lb.)
- 1 large red bell pepper, cut into thin strips
- 16 thin deli ham slices (about ½ lb.)
- 12 fresh basil leaves
- 8 Bibb lettuce leaves

1 Stir together first 3 ingredients.

2 Spread 1 side of each bread slice generously with mayonnaise mixture. Layer cheese, bell pepper strips, ham, basil, and lettuce on half of bread slices. Top with remaining bread slices, mayonnaise mixture sides down. Cut sandwiches in half.

Express Sandwiches

GIANT HAM-AND-PEPPER SALAD SANDWICH

Be sure to bring your appetite to feast on this large sandwich.

Express Sandwiches

SERVES 4

1   (16-oz.) round Italian bread loaf
3   Tbsp. honey mustard
½   cup chive-and-onion cream cheese, softened
1   Tbsp. mayonnaise
1   lb. deli ham, thinly sliced
¼   cup pickled sliced banana peppers, drained
1   (6-oz.) package Swiss cheese slices
4   (1-oz.) American cheese slices
Tomato slices
Lettuce leaves

1 Cut bread loaf in half lengthwise. Spread cut side of top with honey mustard; set aside.

2 Scoop out soft center of remaining bread, leaving a ¼-inch-thick shell. (Reserve soft center of loaf for other uses, if desired.)

3 Stir together cream cheese and mayonnaise; spread in bottom of bread shell. Layer with ham and next 5 ingredients; cover with bread top, honey mustard-side down. Cut into 4 wedges to serve.

INSTANT ADD

Serving sandwiches with chips on the side doesn't have to be dull. Look for multi-colored vegetable chips for extra flavor!

Total time:
15 minutes

**A GIANT
SANDWICH
TO SERVE 4!**

Total time:
20 minutes

USE VERY THINLY
SLICED HAM.

COUNTRY HAM-AND-PEACH PANINI

A hot panini press not only toasts the bread—it also melts the fontina cheese, sealing in the peaches.

SERVES 4

8   ciabatta bread slices*

4   tsp. coarse-grained Dijon mustard

Freshly ground black pepper

4   (1-oz.) fontina cheese slices

4   oz. thinly sliced country ham, prosciutto, or serrano ham

2   medium peaches (about ¾ lb.), unpeeled and sliced

4   tsp. honey (optional)

1   Tbsp. extra virgin olive oil

1 Spread each of 4 bread slices with 1 tsp. mustard, and sprinkle with desired amount of freshly ground pepper. Layer with cheese, ham, peaches, and, if desired, honey. Top with remaining bread slices, and press together gently. Brush sandwiches with oil.

2 Cook sandwiches, in batches, in a preheated panini press 3 to 4 minutes or until golden brown and cheese is melted. (Or use a preheated nonstick grill pan, and cook sandwiches over medium heat 3 to 4 minutes on each side.) Serve immediately.

*Any firm white bread may be substituted.

Express Sandwiches

DAGWOOD SANDWICHES

A Dagwood sandwich, made popular by the comic strip character Dagwood Bumstead, is characterized by layers of meats and cheeses.

Express Sandwiches

SERVES 4

¼ cup mayonnaise

1 Tbsp. Dijon mustard

2 tsp. dill pickle relish

4 (1-oz.) slices 10-grain bread, cut in half diagonally

4 small lettuce leaves

8 slices tomato

3 oz. thinly sliced deli roasted turkey breast

2 (0.7-oz.) slices Cheddar cheese, cut in half

3 oz. thinly sliced deli Black Forest ham

2 (¾-oz.) slices Swiss cheese, cut in half

8 thinly sliced green bell pepper rings

16 thin slices cucumber

4 pimiento-stuffed Spanish olives (optional)

4 wooden picks

1 Combine first 3 ingredients. Spread about 1 Tbsp. mayonnaise mixture on 1 side of each of 4 bread triangles. Top with 1 lettuce leaf, 2 tomato slices, ¾ oz. turkey, 1 Cheddar cheese slice, ¾ oz. ham, 1 Swiss cheese slice, 2 bell pepper rings, and 4 cucumber slices. Cover sandwiches with remaining bread triangles.

2 Thread 1 olive, if desired, onto each of 4 long wooden picks; secure sandwiches with picks.

Total time:
20 minutes

JARRED ITALIAN
OLIVE SALAD
MAKES IT QUICK.

MUFFULETTA

For a make-ahead twist, wrap the sandwich tightly with plastic wrap, and chill under the weight of a heavy cast-iron skillet up to 8 hours.

SERVES 6

- 1 (16-oz.) ciabatta bread loaf
- 1 cup jarred Italian olive salad, drained
- 3 Tbsp. coarse-grained Dijon mustard
- ½ lb. thinly sliced deli porchetta
- 1 (4-oz.) package thinly sliced Italian chorizo
- 1 (3-oz.) package thinly sliced prosciutto
- 8 (1-oz.) provolone cheese slices
- ⅓ cup sliced red onion
- 2 cups loosely packed arugula

1 Cut ciabatta loaf in half lengthwise. Scoop out soft bread from both halves, leaving a ½-inch-thick shell. (Reserve soft center of loaf for another use, if desired.)

2 Spoon olive salad into bottom half of bread loaf, and spread mustard on top half. Layer meats and cheese slices on top of olive mixture. Top with onions and arugula. Cover with bread top, mustard side down. Cut loaf into 6 slices.

Express Sandwiches

SLAW REUBENS

Classic Reuben ingredients combine with some unexpected elements like Granny Smith apple in these griddled sandwiches.

Express
Sandwiches

SERVES 2

- 2 **cups shredded coleslaw mix**
- 5 **Tbsp. Thousand Island dressing, divided**
- 1 **Tbsp. white vinegar**
- ¼ **tsp. freshly ground black pepper**
- 1 **tsp. spicy brown mustard**
- 4 **rye or pumpernickel bread slices**
- 1 **(7-oz.) package shaved roast beef**
- ½ **Granny Smith apple, cored and thinly sliced**
- 2 **(1-oz.) Swiss cheese slices**
- 2 **Tbsp. butter, melted**

1 Stir together coleslaw mix, 2 Tbsp. dressing, vinegar, and black pepper in a medium bowl.

2 Stir together spicy brown mustard and remaining 3 Tbsp. dressing; spread dressing mixture evenly on 1 side of bread slices. Top each of 2 bread slices evenly with beef, apple slices, and cheese slices. Divide slaw mixture evenly over cheese. Top with remaining bread slices, dressing mixture sides down. Brush both sides of sandwiches evenly with melted butter.

3 Cook sandwiches in a large lightly greased nonstick skillet over medium-high heat 2 minutes on each side or until golden. Serve immediately.

Total time:
14 minutes

YOU CAN SUBSTITUTE
CORNED BEEF FOR
ROAST BEEF.

Total time:
15 minutes

**MAKE THE PIMIENTO
CHEESE AHEAD AND
REFRIGERATE.**

ROAST BEEF SUBS

These hearty subs are filled with sliced beef, tomatoes, and pimiento cheese. It's our Southern take on a roast beef sandwich.

SERVES 4

- ½ cup (2 oz.) shredded Cheddar cheese
- ⅓ cup diced red bell pepper
- ¼ cup diced red onion
- ¼ cup bottled Caesar dressing
- 4 (6½-inch) hoagie rolls
- 4 red leaf lettuce leaves
- 8 (¼-inch-thick) tomato slices
- 8 (1-oz.) lean cooked roast beef slices

1 Combine first 4 ingredients in a medium bowl.

2 Cut a ¼-inch-thick slice off top of each roll; set tops aside. Scoop out soft bread of rolls, leaving ½-inch-thick shells. (Reserve soft bread center of rolls for another use, if desired.) Place 1 lettuce leaf in bottom portion of each roll. Spoon cheese mixture over lettuce; top each serving with 2 tomato slices and 2 slices roast beef. Cover with roll tops.

EASY SIDE

Carrot Slaw: Combine 4 tsp. rice wine vinegar; 2 tsp. grated fresh ginger; 2 tsp. olive oil; ½ tsp. salt; ½ tsp. freshly ground pepper; and 4 garlic cloves, minced, in a medium bowl. Add 2 cups matchstick carrots, ½ cup shredded radishes, and 2 Tbsp. chopped fresh cilantro; toss to coat.

LAMB PITA POCKETS

By using leftover grilled lamb, you can make this recipe even easier, plus, your leftovers will take on a whole new vibrant life in these pitas.

Express Sandwiches

🍲 SERVES 4

- 2½ cups diced cooked lamb
- 1   Tbsp. olive oil
- 1½ cups chopped romaine lettuce
- ¼   cup crumbled feta cheese
- 2   small tomatoes, sliced
- 3   Tbsp. bottled Greek dressing
- 4   whole wheat pita rounds, halved and warmed

Yogurt Sauce

1 Sauté lamb in hot olive oil in a medium skillet over high heat 2 minutes or until hot. Combine romaine lettuce, feta cheese, tomatoes, and Greek dressing. Divide lamb among pita rounds. Top with lettuce mixture and Yogurt Sauce.

YOGURT SAUCE

- 1   cup Greek yogurt
- ⅓   cup loosely packed fresh mint leaves, finely chopped
- ¼   cup sour cream
- 1   garlic clove, pressed
- 1   Tbsp. fresh lemon juice
- 1   medium cucumber, peeled, seeded, and chopped
- 1   tsp. kosher salt

1 Stir together yogurt, mint, sour cream, garlic, lemon juice, cucumber, and salt. Serve immediately, or chill and refrigerate up to 2 days.

Total time:
15 minutes

FOR A TWIST,
TURN THESE
INTO WRAPS!

1
original recipe
VEGETABLE QUESADILLAS

 **SERVES 2**

- 1 cup sliced yellow squash*
- ½ cup sliced fresh mushrooms
- ½ cup chopped onion
- ¼ cup chopped green bell pepper
- ½ tsp. table salt
- ¼ tsp. pepper
- ½ tsp. hot sauce
- 2 Tbsp. olive oil
- ½ cup (2 oz.) shredded mozzarella cheese
- ½ cup (2 oz.) shredded Cheddar cheese
- 2 (8-inch) soft taco-size flour tortillas

Jarred salsa

1 Sauté first 7 ingredients in hot oil in a large skillet over medium-high heat 3 to 4 minutes or until tender. Remove vegetables to paper towels to drain, reserving oil in skillet.

2 Place 2 Tbsp. mozzarella cheese and 2 Tbsp. Cheddar cheese on half of each tortilla; top each with half of vegetable mixture and remaining cheeses. Fold tortillas over filling.

3 Cook quesadillas in reserved hot oil in skillet over medium heat 3 to 5 minutes on each side or until light golden. Serve immediately with salsa.

* 1 cup frozen sliced yellow squash, thawed, may be substituted.

Total time:
20 minutes

SIMPLE SWAPS MAKE GREEK, FRENCH, AND ITALIAN TWISTS!

2

FETA CHEESE + KALAMATA OLIVES + BASIL =

GREEK QUESADILLAS

Prepare Vegetable Quesadillas as directed, omitting yellow squash and salsa and substituting crumbled feta for Cheddar. Add 1 Tbsp. chopped Kalamata olives (2 Tbsp. total) and 3 fresh basil leaves to each tortilla along with cheese.

3

COOKED CHICKEN + DELI HAM =

CORDON BLEU QUESADILLAS

Prepare Vegetable Quesadillas as directed, omitting yellow squash, green bell pepper, and salsa. Add 2 Tbsp. chopped cooked chicken (¼ cup total) and 1 slice deli ham to each tortilla along with cheese.

Express Sandwiches

4

GREEN BELL PEPPER + MOZZARELLA CHEESE + PEPPERONI =

PIZZA QUESADILLAS

Prepare Vegetable Quesadillas as directed, omitting yellow squash and Cheddar, increasing green bell pepper to ½ cup, and increasing mozzarella to 1 cup. Add 2 Tbsp. sliced pepperonis (¼ cup total) to each tortilla along with cheese. Substitute pizza sauce for salsa.

Total time:
15 minutes

CHAR TORTILLAS ON THE GRILL FOR A SMOKY FLAVOR.

FRIED CHICKEN TACOS WITH JALAPEÑO-RANCH SAUCE

Use this creamy sauce to dress up store-bought fried chicken or as a salad dressing or dip for wings. Adjust the heat by adding more or less jalapeño. We like to double up on the tortillas, taco-truck style, for these tacos.

 **SERVES 6**

- 1 **cup refrigerated light Ranch dressing**
- 1 **large jalapeño pepper, stemmed**
- 1 **bunch fresh cilantro (about 1½ cups loosely packed)**
- 2 **garlic cloves, chopped**
- 1 **Tbsp. fresh lime juice**
- 12 **fried chicken breast tenders**
- 24 **(6-inch) corn tortillas, warmed**

Sliced radishes

1. Process Ranch dressing, jalapeño pepper, cilantro, garlic, and lime juice in a blender or food processor 2 to 3 seconds or until smooth, stopping to scrape down sides as needed.

2. Place 1 fried chicken breast tender in 2 stacked warmed corn tortillas; repeat with remaining chicken and tortillas. Serve with dressing mixture and sliced radishes.

Express Sandwiches

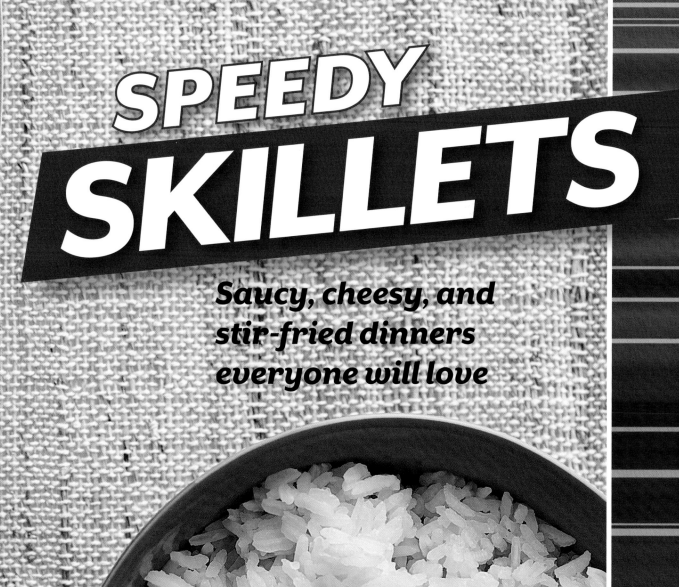

SPEEDY SKILLETS

Saucy, cheesy, and stir-fried dinners everyone will love

Total time:
15 minutes

**CHOOSE A WIDE
PASTA TO SOAK UP
ALL THE FLAVORS.**

ZUCCHINI-MINT PASTA

 **SERVES 4-6**

2 Tbsp. butter

2 Tbsp. olive oil

2 shallots, diced

1½ lb. small zucchini, sliced

1 garlic clove, minced

2 Tbsp. fresh lemon juice

2 tsp. lemon zest

1 tsp. kosher salt

½ tsp. freshly ground black pepper

1 (8.8-oz.) package pappardelle pasta, cooked, or 1 (9-oz.) package refrigerated fettuccine pasta, cooked

½ cup thinly sliced fresh mint

½ cup chopped toasted walnuts

¼ cup freshly grated Parmesan cheese

4 oz. crumbled feta cheese

1 Melt butter with olive oil in a large nonstick skillet over medium-high heat; add shallots, and sauté 2 minutes. Add zucchini; sauté 5 minutes or until zucchini is tender. Stir in minced garlic, and cook 1 minute. Remove from heat; stir in lemon juice, lemon zest, kosher salt, and freshly ground black pepper.

2 Toss in cooked pasta, fresh mint, walnuts, and Parmesan cheese. Sprinkle with feta cheese just before serving.

Speedy Skillets

1

original recipe

EASY SKILLET PIMIENTO MAC 'N' CHEESE

 **SERVES 6**

- ½ (16-oz.) package penne pasta
- 2 Tbsp. all-purpose flour
- 1½ cups 1% low-fat milk
- 1 cup (4 oz.) shredded sharp Cheddar cheese
- 1 (4-oz.) jar diced pimiento, drained
- ¾ tsp. table salt
- ¼ tsp. pepper

Pinch of paprika

1 Prepare pasta according to package directions.

2 Whisk together flour and ¼ cup milk. Add flour mixture to remaining milk, whisking until smooth.

3 Bring milk mixture to a boil in a large skillet over medium heat; reduce heat to medium-low, and simmer, whisking constantly, 3 to 5 minutes or until smooth. Stir in cheese and next 4 ingredients until smooth. Stir in pasta, and cook 1 minute or until thoroughly heated. Serve immediately.

Total time: **20 minutes**

THE BEST PART: IT'S BASICALLY A ONE-POT DISH!

2

FONTINA CHEESE + TOMATOES + BASIL + PARMESAN CHEESE =

ITALIANO
MAC 'N' CHEESE

Prepare Easy Skillet Pimiento Mac 'n' Cheese as
directed, substituting fontina cheese
for Cheddar and 1 cup chopped tomatoes for
pimientos. Top with fresh basil and
grated Parmesan cheese.

3

WHITE AMERICAN CHEESE + GREEN CHILES =

QUESO DIP
MAC 'N' CHEESE

Prepare Easy Skillet Pimiento Mac 'n' Cheese as
directed, substituting white American cheese
for Cheddar and 1 (4-oz.) can green chiles,
undrained, for pimentos.

Speedy
Skillets

4

SMOKED PORK + BARBECUE SAUCE =

BBQ
MAC 'N' CHEESE

Prepare Easy Skillet Pimiento Mac 'n' Cheese
as directed, omitting pimientos. Stir in 2 cups
shredded smoked pork, and top each serving
with a drizzle of bottle barbecue sauce.

**Total time:
20 minutes**

**COOK RICE THE
NIGHT BEFORE TO
SAVE TIME.**

CURRIED SHRIMP WITH PEANUTS

Cooking the curry powder with the flour brings out the essential oils, making the dish more flavorful.

SERVES 4-6

- 2 Tbsp. butter
- 1 Tbsp. all-purpose flour
- 2 tsp. curry powder
- ¾ cup milk
- ¾ cup chicken broth
- ⅓ cup ketchup
- 1 Tbsp. grated fresh ginger
- ½ jalapeño pepper, seeded and chopped
- ¼ tsp. dried crushed red pepper (optional)
- 2½ lb. peeled large, raw shrimp, deveined
- 2 tsp. fresh lime juice
- ¼ tsp. kosher salt

Cooked white rice

Toppings: salted cocktail peanuts, bean sprouts, toasted unsweetened flaked coconut, cilantro

1 Melt butter in a heavy saucepan over low heat; whisk in flour and curry powder until smooth. Cook, whisking constantly, 1 minute. Gradually whisk in milk, next 4 ingredients, and, if desired, dried crushed red pepper. Increase heat to medium, and cook, whisking constantly, 5 to 6 minutes or until mixture is thickened and bubbly.

2 Stir in shrimp, lime juice, and salt. Reduce heat to medium-low, and cook, stirring often, 5 minutes or just until shrimp turn pink. Serve over rice with desired toppings.

Speedy Skillets

SHRIMP SCAMPI

Serve this coastal dish with toasted French bread baguette slices or warm angel hair pasta. It's a winner either way.

 SERVES 2

1½ lb. peeled jumbo raw shrimp (16/20 count)*

1½ Tbsp. jarred minced garlic

1½ Tbsp. olive oil

¼ cup finely chopped fresh flat-leaf parsley

1½ Tbsp. fresh lemon juice

½ tsp. table salt

Dash of ground red pepper

1 Devein shrimp, if desired.

2 Sauté garlic in hot oil in a medium-size nonstick skillet over medium-high heat 1 minute.

3 Add shrimp to skillet, and cook, stirring occasionally, 5 minutes or just until shrimp turn pink.

4 Remove skillet from heat; stir in parsley and remaining ingredients.

* 2¼ lb. unpeeled jumbo raw shrimp may be substituted. Peel shrimp prior to cooking.

Speedy Skillets

EASY SIDE

Simple Caesar Salad: Toss 1 (6-oz.) bag chopped romaine lettuce with ¼ cup bottled Caesar dressing. Sprinkle with ¼ cup shaved Parmesan and ½ cup croutons. Serve with additional dressing.

Total time:
10 minutes

SEVEN INGREDIENTS
MAKE FOR A
FAST DINNER.

Total time:
20 minutes

USE 2½ CUPS LEFTOVER RICE IF YOU HAVE SOME!

SHRIMP FRIED RICE

 SERVES 4

2   (3.5-oz.) bags quick-cooking long-grain rice
3   Tbsp. canola oil, divided
2   large eggs, lightly beaten
1   tsp. jarred minced garlic
¼   tsp. crushed red pepper
1   lb. peeled and deveined frozen raw shrimp, thawed
1½ cups frozen mixed vegetables, thawed
3   Tbsp. soy sauce

1 Cook rice according to package directions; set aside.

2 Meanwhile, place 1 Tbsp. oil in a large skillet over medium-high heat. Add eggs; cook 1 to 2 minutes, stirring frequently until scrambled. Remove from skillet, and set aside.

3 Heat remaining 2 Tbsp. oil in skillet; add garlic, crushed red pepper, and shrimp. Cook 2 minutes or until shrimp turn pink. Add vegetables, and cook until thoroughly heated. Stir in soy sauce, reserved rice, and scrambled eggs; cook 1 minute or until thoroughly heated.

EASY SIDE

Edamame: Microwave frozen edamame according to package directions. Serve with soy sauce or sprinkle with sea salt. Serve hot.

FRIED CATFISH WITH PICKLED PEPPERS

 SERVES 4

1½ cups all-purpose flour

2¼ tsp. table salt, divided

2 tsp. freshly ground black pepper, divided

4 large eggs

1½ cups plain yellow cornmeal

4 (6-oz.) catfish fillets

Vegetable oil

Garnishes: jarred pickled pepper slices, cracked black pepper, sea salt

1 Combine flour and 1 tsp. each salt and pepper in a shallow dish. Whisk together eggs and 2 Tbsp. water in another dish. Combine cornmeal, 1 tsp. salt, and remaining 1 tsp. pepper in a third dish. Sprinkle catfish with remaining ¼ tsp. salt. Dredge fillets, 1 at a time, in flour mixture, shaking off excess; dip in egg mixture, and dredge in cornmeal mixture, shaking off excess. Place on a wire rack in a jelly-roll pan.

2 Pour oil to depth of 2 inches in a cast-iron Dutch oven. Heat over medium-high heat to 350°. Fry fillets, 2 at a time, in hot oil 6 minutes or until done. Drain on a wire rack over paper towels.

Speedy Skillets

Total time:
20 minutes

LOOK FOR PICKLED PEPPERS IN THE PICKLE AISLE.

Total time:
20 minutes

THIN CUTLETS COOK QUICKLY, AS DOES THE SAUCE.

CHICKEN CUTLETS WITH PECAN SAUCE

 SERVES 4

4   chicken cutlets (about 1¼ lb.)
1   tsp. table salt
½   tsp. pepper
3   Tbsp. all-purpose flour
3   Tbsp. olive oil
½   cup toasted pecan halves
½   cup chicken broth
1   Tbsp. brown sugar
2   Tbsp. cider vinegar
½   tsp. dried thyme
2   Tbsp. butter
Garnish: fresh thyme

1 Sprinkle chicken with salt and pepper. Dredge in flour.

2 Cook chicken in hot oil in skillet over medium heat 3 to 4 minutes on each side or until golden brown and done. Transfer to a serving platter. Top with pecans.

3 Add chicken broth to skillet, and cook 2 minutes, stirring to loosen particles from bottom of skillet. Add brown sugar, vinegar, and dried thyme, and cook 3 to 4 minutes or until sugar is melted and sauce is slightly thickened. Whisk in remaining 2 Tbsp. butter. Serve sauce over chicken.

EASY SIDE

Garlic-Pepper Mixed Vegetables: Cook 1 (11-oz.) package frozen steam-in-bag mixed vegetables according to package directions. Toss with 1 tsp. freshly ground garlic-pepper seasoning.

Speedy Skillets

EASY SKILLET CORDON BLEU

 SERVES 4

½ cup Italian-seasoned breadcrumbs

1 tsp. pepper

½ tsp. table salt

8 chicken tenders (about 1 lb.)

1 Tbsp. butter

1 Tbsp. olive oil

8 Canadian bacon slices, cut into thin strips

4 (¾- or 1-oz.) Swiss cheese slices, halved

Garnish: chopped fresh parsley

1 Preheat broiler with oven rack 5½ inches from heat. Combine breadcrumbs and next 2 ingredients in a large zip-top plastic freezer bag. Add chicken to freezer bag. Seal bag, and shake to coat.

2 Melt butter with oil in an ovenproof skillet over medium heat. Cook chicken 3½ to 4 minutes on each side or until done. Arrange Canadian bacon strips over chicken in skillet, and top each with 1 cheese slice half. Broil 2 minutes or until cheese is melted.

Speedy Skillets

EASY SIDE

Roasted Broccoli: Preheat oven to 475°. Cut 1¼ lb. broccoli into 3-inch-long spears; cut thick stems in half lengthwise. Place in a single layer on a well-greased jelly-roll pan. Combine 1 Tbsp. olive oil and 1 garlic clove, pressed; drizzle broccoli with oil mixture, and toss well. Sprinkle with salt and pepper to taste. Bake for 14 minutes. Sprinkle toasted sliced almonds over broccoli.

Total time:
20 minutes

YOU CAN ALSO USE
CHICKEN BREASTS
CUT INTO STRIPS.

Total time:
20 minutes

SALTINE CRACKERS MAKE FOR A CRISPY COATING!

CHICKEN-FRIED STEAK

Crispy, crunchy cubed steak topped with Cream Gravy is the ultimate comfort food. Serve alongside steamed green beans and prepared refrigerated mashed potatoes for a complete meal.

SERVES 6

- 6 (4-oz.) cubed steaks (1½ lb.)
- ½ tsp. table salt
- ½ tsp. pepper
- ¼ cup all-purpose flour
- ½ cup egg substitute
- 45 saltine crackers, crushed (1 sleeve plus 7 crackers)

Vegetable cooking spray

Cream Gravy

CREAM GRAVY

- 1½ cups 1% low-fat milk
- ¼ cup all-purpose flour
- 1 Tbsp. lower-sodium jarred chicken soup base
- ½ tsp. pepper

1 Sprinkle steaks with salt and pepper. Dredge steaks in flour; dip in egg substitute, and dredge in crushed crackers. Lightly coat steaks on each side with cooking spray.

2 Cook steaks, in batches, in a hot nonstick skillet over medium heat 3 to 4 minutes on each side or until golden, turning twice. Transfer steaks to a wire rack in a jelly-roll pan. Keep warm in a 225° oven. Serve with Cream Gravy.

1 Gradually whisk milk into flour until smooth; cook over medium heat, whisking constantly, 3 to 5 minutes or until mixture is thickened and bubbly. Whisk in soup base and pepper.

Speedy Skillets

TURKEY TETRAZZINI

 SERVES 2

1½ cups diced deli turkey breast (about ½ lb.)*

½ cup chopped onion

Cooking spray

¼ cup milk

1 (10¾-oz.) can cream of mushroom soup

¾ cup (3 oz.) shredded sharp Cheddar cheese

4 oz. spaghetti, cooked

2 Tbsp. chopped fresh parsley

⅛ tsp. pepper

1 (2-oz.) jar diced pimiento, drained

1 Sauté turkey and onion in a large nonstick skillet coated with cooking spray over medium-high heat 3 minutes or until onion is tender.

2 Stir in milk, soup, and cheese; reduce heat to low, and cook, stirring constantly, 4 minutes or until cheese melts and mixture is smooth. Stir in spaghetti and remaining ingredients; cook 2 to 3 minutes or until thoroughly heated.

* Diced ham may be substituted.

INSTANT ADD

Serve this creamy pasta dish alongside a green vegetable, or pump up the flavor of this recipe by stirring in ⅓ cup frozen peas along with spaghetti.

Total time:
18 minutes

TRY THIS WITH DICED DELI HAM OR CHICKEN INSTEAD.

Total time:
20 minutes

WHILE PASTA BOILS, MAKE THE CHEESE SAUCE.

QUICK-START BACON-CHEDDAR MAC 'N' CHEESE

Rather than purchasing shredded cheese, shred the cheese from a block to ensure good melting. You'll still have dinner on the table in no time thanks to a microwave-cooked sauce.

 SERVES 9

1⅔ cups uncooked elbow macaroni

1 (12-oz.) can evaporated milk

1 (8-oz.) block extra-sharp Cheddar cheese, shredded

6 oz. pasteurized prepared cheese product, cubed

2 oz. cream cheese, cubed

¼ tsp. freshly ground black pepper

¼ cup sliced green onions

6 cooked bacon slices, crumbled

1 Prepare pasta according to package directions.

2 Meanwhile, combine evaporated milk, cheeses, and black pepper in a large microwave-safe bowl. Microwave at MEDIUM (50% power) 8 minutes or until cheeses melt, stirring every 3 minutes.

3 Stir pasta into cheese sauce; sprinkle with green onions and bacon. Serve immediately.

Speedy Skillets

PORK-AND-GREEN BEAN STIR-FRY

The key to this dish is developing a nice char on the green beans. To do so, heat the oil in your skillet until it almost smokes before adding the beans. Let them sear, stirring every 20 to 30 seconds, and they'll take on color.

 SERVES 4

1½ lb. ground pork

2 garlic cloves, thinly sliced

½ tsp. table salt

¼ tsp. ground red pepper

1 (8-oz.) package haricots verts (thin green beans)

1 Tbsp. peanut oil or vegetable oil

¾ cup triple-ginger or regular teriyaki sauce

½ tsp. loosely packed lime zest

1 Tbsp. fresh lime juice

Hot cooked rice or thin rice noodles

Garnishes: thinly sliced red jalapeño pepper, lime halves

1 Brown ground pork and next 3 ingredients in a large stainless steel skillet over medium-high heat, stirring often, 7 to 8 minutes or until meat crumbles and is no longer pink; drain. Wipe skillet clean.

2 Cook green beans in hot oil in skillet over medium-high heat, stirring occasionally, 4 to 5 minutes or until just tender and slightly charred.

3 Stir together teriyaki sauce and next 2 ingredients.

4 Stir pork mixture into green beans. Stir in teriyaki mixture, tossing to coat. Serve immediately over rice or noodles.

Note: We tested with Kikkoman Triple Ginger Takumi Collection Teriyaki Sauce.

Speedy Skillets

Total time:
20 minutes

**TAME THE HEAT
WITH BELL PEPPERS
INSTEAD OF CHILES.**

SKILLET SHEPHERD'S PIE

Packaged products and a one-pot method make this hearty meal a weeknight staple.

 SERVES 4

- 1 lb. ground round
- ¾ cup chopped onion
- 2 garlic cloves, minced
- 2 Tbsp. all-purpose flour
- ¾ cup beef broth
- 1 Tbsp. tomato paste
- ½ tsp. table salt
- ½ tsp. freshly ground black pepper
- 2 tsp. chopped fresh thyme
- 1 cup frozen peas and carrots
- 1 (24-oz.) package refrigerated mashed potatoes
- ¾ cup (3 oz.) shredded sharp Cheddar cheese

1 Cook ground beef, onion, and garlic in a medium-size nonstick skillet over medium-high heat, stirring often, 5 minutes until meat crumbles and is no longer pink; drain and return to skillet.

2 Sprinkle beef mixture with flour; cook, stirring constantly, 1 minute. Add broth and next 4 ingredients, stirring until blended. Stir in peas and carrots; bring to a boil. Cover, reduce heat to low, and simmer, stirring occasionally, 8 minutes or until slightly thickened.

3 Meanwhile, heat mashed potatoes according to package directions.

4 Spoon mashed potatoes over beef mixture, spreading almost to edge of skillet; sprinkle with cheese. Cover and simmer 2 minutes or until cheese melts.

Speedy Skillets

BEEF-AND-BRUSSELS SPROUTS STIR-FRY

Substitute any cruciferous vegetable cut into even pieces in place of Brussels sprouts, from broccoli and cauliflower to cabbage and bok choy.

 SERVES 4

½ lb. flank steak

¼ tsp. table salt

⅛ tsp. freshly ground black pepper

2 Tbsp. peanut oil, divided

½ cup beef broth or water

1 Tbsp. light brown sugar

2 Tbsp. soy sauce

2 tsp. fresh lime juice

½ tsp. cornstarch

12 oz. fresh Brussels sprouts, trimmed and halved

1 red jalapeño or red serrano pepper, sliced

1 Tbsp. grated fresh ginger

2 garlic cloves, thinly sliced

¼ cup chopped fresh mint

Hot cooked rice

1 Cut steak diagonally across the grain into thin strips. Sprinkle with salt and pepper.

2 Stir-fry steak, in 2 batches, in 1 Tbsp. hot oil in a large cast-iron or stainless steel skillet over high heat 2 to 3 minutes or until meat is no longer pink. Transfer steak to a plate, and wipe skillet clean.

3 Whisk together beef broth and next 4 ingredients in a small bowl until smooth.

4 Stir-fry Brussels sprouts in remaining 1 Tbsp. hot oil over high heat 2 minutes or until lightly browned. Add jalapeño pepper, ginger, and garlic, and stir-fry 1 minute. Pour soy sauce mixture over Brussels sprouts, and bring mixture to a boil. Cook, stirring often, 3 to 4 minutes or until sprouts are tender. Stir in mint and steak. Serve over rice.

Total time:
20 minutes

FLANK STEAK,
CUT THINLY, COOKS
EVENLY AND QUICKLY.

SIMPLE SUPPERS

Easy dinnertime favorites like ravioli, crab cakes, grilled chicken, and steaks

Total time:
20 minutes

CAKES MIX UP
EASILY WITH
JUST A FORK.

BLACK-EYED PEA CAKES WITH HEIRLOOM TOMATOES AND SLAW

SERVES 6

1   (15-oz.) can seasoned black-eyed peas, undrained

2   garlic cloves, pressed

1   (6-oz.) package buttermilk cornbread mix

1   large egg, lightly beaten

¼   cup sour cream

1½ tsp. Southwest chipotle salt-free seasoning blend

1   tsp. table salt, divided

⅓   cup sour cream

1   tsp. lime zest

1   Tbsp. fresh lime juice

2   tsp. sugar

1   (12-oz.) package fresh broccoli slaw

2   large heirloom tomatoes, cut into ¼-inch-thick slices

1 Coarsely mash peas with fork. Stir in garlic, next 4 ingredients, and ½ tsp. salt. Stir until blended.

2 Spoon about ⅓ cup batter for each cake onto a hot lightly greased griddle. Cook cakes 2 minutes or until edges look dry and cooked; turn and cook 2 more minutes.

3 Stir together ⅓ cup sour cream, next 3 ingredients, and remaining ½ tsp. salt in a large bowl. Stir in slaw.

4 Place 2 cooked cakes on a serving plate; top cakes with 2 tomato slices. Add salt and pepper to taste. Top with slaw; serve immediately.

Simple Suppers

SPICY FISH TACOS

 SERVES 2-4

- 6 (6-oz.) flounder fillets
- 1 lime
- 2 Tbsp. chili powder
- 2 tsp. table salt
- 2 tsp. ground cumin
- ½ tsp. ground red pepper
- 1½ cups plain yellow cornmeal

Vegetable oil

- 6 (8-inch) soft taco-size flour or corn tortillas, warmed

Mango Salsa

Refrigerated guacamole

Toppings: shredded iceberg lettuce, chopped tomato

Garnishes: lime wedges, fresh cilantro leaves

1 Place fish in a shallow dish. Squeeze juice from lime over fillets. Combine chili powder and next 3 ingredients. Sprinkle 1½ Tbsp. seasoning mixture evenly over fish, coating both sides of fillets. Reserve remaining seasoning mixture.

2 Combine cornmeal and reserved seasoning mixture in a shallow dish. Dredge fish fillets in cornmeal mixture, shaking off excess.

3 Pour oil to depth of 1½ inches in a Dutch oven; heat to 350°. Fry fillets, in batches, 2 to 3 minutes or until golden brown. Drain fillets on wire racks over paper towels.

4 Break each fillet into chunks, using a fork. Place fish in warmed tortillas, and serve with Mango Salsa, guacamole, and desired toppings.

MANGO SALSA

- 1 mango, chopped
- 1 jalapeño, seeded and finely chopped
- 1 garlic clove, minced
- 1 Tbsp. fresh lime juice
- 1 Tbsp. finely chopped red onion
- 1 Tbsp. chopped fresh cilantro
- ¼ tsp. table salt

1 Stir together all ingredients. Cover and chill until ready to serve. Makes 1 cup.

Simple
Suppers

**Total time:
20 minutes**

FLAVORFUL FISH
IN A FLASH, THANKS
TO THE GRILL.

GRILLED GROUPER WITH WATERMELON SALSA

Choose firm, symmetrical, unblemished watermelons without cracks or soft spots. When buying precut watermelon, look for deep color, firm flesh, and a sweet fragrance.

 **SERVES 4**

- 4 (4-oz.) grouper fillets
- 1 tsp. freshly ground pepper
- 1 tsp. table salt, divided
- 3 Tbsp. olive oil, divided
- 2 cups chopped seedless watermelon
- ¼ cup chopped pitted kalamata olives
- ½ English cucumber, chopped
- 1 small jalapeño pepper, seeded and minced
- 2 Tbsp. minced red onion
- 2 Tbsp. white balsamic vinegar

1 Preheat grill to 350° to 400° (medium-high) heat. Sprinkle fillets with pepper and ½ tsp. salt. Drizzle with 2 Tbsp. olive oil.

2 Grill fish, covered with grill lid, 3 to 4 minutes on each side or just until fish flakes with a fork and is opaque in center.

3 Combine chopped watermelon, next 5 ingredients, remaining ½ tsp. salt, and remaining 1 Tbsp. olive oil. Serve with grilled fish.

Simple Suppers

CRUNCHY CRAB CAKES

 **SERVES 8**

1 (16-oz.) package fresh lump crabmeat, drained

2 large lemons

1 (4-oz.) jar diced pimiento, well drained

2 green onions, chopped

1 large egg, lightly beaten

2 Tbsp. mayonnaise

1 tsp. Old Bay seasoning

2 tsp. Dijon mustard

1 cup panko (Japanese breadcrumbs), divided

¼ cup canola oil

Garnishes: lemon zest, sliced green onions, sour cream

1 Pick crabmeat, removing any bits of shell.

2 Grate zest from lemons to equal 2 tsp.; cut lemons in half, and squeeze juice to equal ¼ cup. Stir together lemon zest and juice, pimiento, and next 5 ingredients until well blended. Gently fold in crabmeat and ½ cup breadcrumbs.

3 Shape mixture into 8 patties. Dredge patties in remaining ½ cup breadcrumbs.

4 Cook half of patties in 2 Tbsp. hot oil in a large nonstick skillet over medium heat 2 minutes on each side or until golden brown; drain on a wire rack. Repeat procedure with remaining oil and patties.

Simple Suppers

 INSTANT ADD

Serve these crab cakes over a salad for a delicious dinner. Or serve them on dinner rolls with lettuce, tomato, and a rémoulade sauce for a tasty slider.

Total time:
20 minutes

**MAKE SMALLER
CAKES FOR QUICK
APPETIZERS.**

Total time:
20 minutes

SHRIMP ARE THE SPEEDIEST SEAFOOD TO COOK.

GRILLED BLACKENED SHRIMP KABOBS

 **SERVES 4-6**

36 unpeeled, large raw shrimp (about 1 lb.)

1 tsp. olive oil

2 tsp. Cajun blackened seasoning

18 (6-inch) wooden skewers

36 fresh blackberries

18 fresh mango slices

Mint-Lime Drizzle

Garnishes: lime wedges, chopped fresh mint

1 Preheat grill to 350° to 400° (medium-high) heat. Peel shrimp, leaving tails on; devein, if desired.

2 Place shrimp in a large bowl, and drizzle with olive oil. Sprinkle with seasoning, and toss to coat.

3 Grill shrimp, covered with grill lid, 2 to 3 minutes on each side or just until shrimp turn pink.

4 Thread each skewer with 2 grilled shrimp, 2 blackberries, and 1 mango slice. Brush with Mint-Lime Drizzle.

MINT-LIME DRIZZLE

1 Tbsp. chopped fresh mint

1 Tbsp. fresh lime juice

1 Tbsp. olive oil

1 tsp. sugar

1 Stir all ingredients together.

GARDEN TOMATO SAUCE OVER PASTA

We love this sauce as a meatless meal over hearty pasta. Or try it in lasagna or on a meatball sub.

SERVES 4-6

- 1 onion, diced (about 1 cup)
- 1 Tbsp. olive oil
- 1 garlic clove, minced
- 4 medium-size heirloom tomatoes (about 2 lb.), cored and chopped
- ¼ cup dry red wine
- 3 Tbsp. chopped fresh oregano or marjoram

Hot cooked pasta

Garnish: fresh oregano leaves

1 Sauté onion in hot oil in a Dutch oven over medium-high heat 3 minutes or until tender. Add garlic; sauté 1 minute. Add tomatoes, kosher salt, and freshly ground pepper to taste.

2 Cook, stirring often, 2 to 3 minutes or until tomatoes start to release their juices. Add wine, and cook, stirring occasionally, 5 to 8 minutes or until almost all liquid evaporates.

3 Remove from heat, and stir in oregano. Serve sauce over hot cooked pasta. Refrigerate sauce in an airtight container up to 1 week, or freeze up to 1 month.

Total time:
15 minutes

GREAT TO MAKE AHEAD— FREEZER READY!

1

original recipe

CHEESE RAVIOLI WITH TOMATOES AND MASCARPONE

SERVES 6

- 1 (24-oz.) package frozen cheese-filled ravioli
- 3 pt. assorted grape tomatoes
- 1 large tomato, chopped
- 2 garlic cloves, chopped
- 2 Tbsp. olive oil
- ¼ cup butter, cubed
- 1 Tbsp. fresh lemon juice
- ¾ tsp. kosher salt
- ¼ tsp. freshly ground black pepper
- ½ cup torn assorted fresh herbs (such as parsley and basil)
- 1 (8-oz.) container mascarpone cheese

1. Prepare pasta according to package directions.

2. Meanwhile, preheat broiler with oven rack 4 to 5 inches from heat. Stir together tomatoes, garlic, and olive oil in a 15- x 10-inch jelly-roll pan.

3. Broil 5 to 8 minutes or until tomatoes are charred, stirring halfway through.

4. Transfer tomato mixture to a large bowl. Stir in butter, next 3 ingredients, and ¼ cup fresh herbs. Spoon over hot cooked ravioli; dollop with cheese. Sprinkle with remaining ¼ cup fresh herbs. Serve immediately.

Note: We tested with Celentano Cheese Ravioli.

Total time: 20 minutes

THE TOMATOES BROIL WHILE THE PASTA COOKS.

2

MUSHROOM-FILLED RAVIOLI + MUSHROOMS =

TRIPLE MUSHROOM RAVIOLI

Prepare Cheese Ravioli with Tomatoes and Mascarpone as directed, substituting mushroom-filled ravioli for the cheese variety. Substitute 2 (8-oz.) packages sliced mushrooms for tomatoes. Top each serving with a couple drops of truffle oil.

3

BUTTERNUT SQUASH =

BUTTERNUT SQUASH RAVIOLI

Prepare Cheese Ravioli with Tomatoes and Mascarpone as directed, substituting 2 cups chopped butternut squash for the tomatoes; toss with oil and bake at 400° for 30 to 35 minutes or until tender (do not broil). Proceed with recipe as directed.

4

SAUSAGE-FILLED RAVIOLI + BACON =

MEAT LOVER'S RAVIOLI

Prepare Cheese Ravioli with Tomatoes and Mascarpone as directed, substituting sausage-filled ravioli for the cheese variety. Omit fresh herbs and top with ½ cup chopped cooked bacon.

PAN-GRILLED CHICKEN WITH FRESH PLUM SALSA

SERVES 4

- 1 cup chopped ripe plums (about 2 plums)
- 1 small jalapeño pepper, seeded and diced
- 2 Tbsp. chopped fresh basil
- 2 Tbsp. chopped red onion
- 2 tsp. fresh lime juice
- ¾ tsp. table salt, divided
- 2 Tbsp. brown sugar
- ½ tsp. ground cumin
- 4 (4-oz.) chicken breast cutlets
- 2 tsp. olive oil

1 Stir together plums, next 4 ingredients, and ¼ tsp. salt in a medium bowl.

2 Stir together brown sugar, cumin, and remaining ½ tsp. salt in a small bowl. Rub chicken with brown sugar mixture.

3 Cook chicken in hot oil in a grill pan or nonstick skillet over medium heat 3 minutes on each side or until done. Serve with plum mixture.

EASY SIDE

Steamed Green Beans: Prepare 1 (12-oz.) package washed and trimmed green beans according to microwave directions on package. Toss with 1 Tbsp. extra virgin olive oil, and sprinkle with salt and pepper to taste.

Simple Suppers

Total time:
15 minutes

PEACHES WORK GREAT, TOO, IF PLUMS ARE UNAVAILABLE.

Total time:
15 minutes

**CHICKEN TENDERS
WORK HERE AND
SAVE TIME, TOO.**

MANGO CHUTNEY-GLAZED CHICKEN SKEWERS

Bottled chutney does double duty as a basting sauce and as a dipping sauce to serve with these little skewers. If you use wooden skewers, be sure to soak them for at least 30 minutes before threading the chicken. This prevents the skewer ends from burning.

 **SERVES 4-5**

1½ tsp. chili powder

¾ tsp. table salt

¼ tsp. ground cumin

Cooking spray

4 (6-oz.) skinned and boned chicken breasts

2 tsp. vegetable oil

16 (6-inch) wooden skewers

1 (9-oz.) bottle mango chutney

1 Combine first 3 ingredients in a small bowl; set aside. Spray cold grill rack with cooking spray. Preheat grill to medium-high (350° to 400°) heat.

2 Place chicken between 2 sheets of heavy-duty plastic wrap, and pound to ½-inch thickness using a meat mallet or rolling pin. Cut each breast half lengthwise into 4 strips. Place chicken strips in a bowl; add chili powder mixture, and toss well to coat chicken. Drizzle chicken with oil.

3 Thread 1 chicken strip onto each of 16 (6-inch) skewers; brush chicken with 3 Tbsp. chutney. Grill chicken, covered, 3 to 4 minutes on each side or until done. Serve with additional chutney.

Simple
Suppers

SESAME CHICKEN AND GARDEN VEGETABLES

Dress a double batch of this light but satisfying dinner with the sesame dressing. The flavors get even better overnight in the fridge, and leftovers make a gourmet on-the-go lunch.

SERVES 4

½ cup reduced-fat sesame dressing

2 Tbsp. fresh lime juice

¼ tsp. dried crushed red pepper

1 (6-oz.) package regular baby or French baby carrots, thinly sliced lengthwise

1 (4-oz.) package fresh sugar snap peas, halved lengthwise

½ English cucumber, thinly sliced into half moons

3 radishes, thinly sliced

2 boneless deli-roasted chicken breasts, sliced

⅓ cup chopped fresh cilantro

2 Tbsp. toasted sesame seeds

1 Whisk together first 3 ingredients; reserve 3 Tbsp.

2 Cook carrots in boiling salted water to cover 2 to 3 minutes or until crisp-tender. Add peas; cook 2 more minutes; drain. Plunge into ice water to stop the cooking process; drain.

3 Toss together dressing mixture, carrot mixture, cucumber, and radishes. Top with chicken and cilantro. Drizzle with reserved 3 Tbsp. dressing mixture. Sprinkle with sesame seeds. Serve immediately, or refrigerate up to 2 days.

Note: We tested with Ken's Steak House Lite Asian Sesame Dressing.

Simple Suppers

Total time:
20 minutes

USING ROTISSERIE
CHICKEN BREAST
MAKES THIS QUICK.

Total time:
15 minutes

USE ½-TO 1-INCH-
THICK PORK CHOPS
SO THEY STAY MOIST.

GRILLED BASIL-AND-GARLIC PORK CHOPS

These thick-grilled chops are easy enough for a weeknight supper, but elegant enough for company. Serve with Basmati Rice and Peas or a baked sweet potato.

 **SERVES 6**

1 tsp. table salt
1 tsp. pepper
1 tsp. dried basil
½ tsp. garlic powder
6 (6- to 8-oz.) bone-in pork loin chops

1 Preheat grill to 350° to 400° (medium-high) heat. Combine first 4 ingredients; sprinkle over pork chops.

2 Grill pork, covered with grill lid, 5 to 7 minutes on each side or until done.

EASY SIDE

Basmati Rice and Peas: Prepare 2 (8.5-oz.) packages heat-and-serve basmati rice according to package directions. Stir in 1 (15½-oz.) can black-eyed peas, drained and rinsed, and 1 ½ tsp. lemon zest, using a fork. Cover and let stand 5 minutes. Sprinkle with 2 green onions, thinly sliced.

PORK CHOPS WITH SHALLOT-CRANBERRY SAUCE

For extra orange flavor, add grated orange peel to the Shallot-Cranberry Sauce.

SERVES 4

- 4 **boneless pork loin chops (¾ inch thick)**
- ¾ **tsp. table salt, divided**
- ½ **tsp. freshly ground pepper**
- 2 **Tbsp. butter, divided**
- 2 **shallots, finely chopped (¼ cup)**
- 1 **(14-oz.) can whole berry cranberry sauce**
- 1 **(8.25-oz.) can mandarin orange segments, drained**
- 1½ **tsp. chopped fresh thyme leaves**

1 Sprinkle both sides of pork chops with ½ tsp. salt and pepper. In a large skillet, melt 1 Tbsp. butter over medium-high heat. Add pork; cook 8 to 10 minutes, turning once, or until meat thermometer inserted in center reads at least 145°. Remove pork from skillet; cover to keep warm.

2 In same skillet, melt remaining 1 Tbsp. butter over medium-high heat. Add shallots; cook 1 to 2 minutes, stirring constantly. Add cranberry sauce, orange segments, and remaining ¼ tsp. salt; heat to boiling. Return pork and any juices to skillet; cook 1 to 2 minutes or until heated. Sprinkle with thyme.

EASY SIDE

Buttery Mashed Potatoes: Heat 1 (24-oz.) package refrigerated mashed potatoes according to package directions. Stir in 2 Tbsp. butter and ¼ tsp. freshly ground black pepper.

Simple Suppers

Total time:
20 minutes

USE CANNED MAN-
DARIN ORANGES AND
CRANBERRY SAUCE.

Total time:
20 minutes

TACO SEASONING
MAKES THIS RECIPE
SO SPEEDY!

SUPREME BEEF TOSTADAS

 **SERVES 6**

1½ lb. lean ground beef

1 small onion, chopped

1 package taco seasoning mix

Peanut oil

6 (8-inch) flour tortillas

1 (15-oz.) can kidney beans, drained and rinsed

1 large tomato, chopped

1 (8-oz.) bag preshredded iceberg lettuce

1 large avocado, peeled and chopped

2 cups (8 oz.) shredded sharp Cheddar cheese

Toppings: sour cream, salsa

1 Cook first 3 ingredients in a large skillet over medium heat, stirring until beef crumbles and is no longer pink; drain and set aside.

2 Pour oil to a depth of ¼ inch into a heavy skillet. Fry tortillas, 1 at a time, in hot oil over high heat 20 seconds on each side or until crisp and golden brown. Drain on paper towels.

3 Layer beef mixture, beans, tomato, and next 3 ingredients evenly on each of warm tortillas. Serve with desired toppings.

Simple
Suppers

GRILLED STEAK WITH PINEAPPLE SALSA

Grilling the pineapple slices and scallions alongside the meat preps them simultaneously for a quick stir into bottled salsa to serve on the top.

 **SERVES 4**

Cooking spray

- 1 (8-oz.) can pineapple slices, drained
- 2 Tbsp. brown sugar
- ½ tsp. kosher salt, divided
- 1 (1-lb.) flat-iron steak
- 2 scallions
- ½ cup chunky salsa

Precooked rice

Garnish: grilled scallions

1 Spray cold grill rack with cooking spray. Preheat grill to medium-high (350° to 400°) heat.

2 Sprinkle pineapple with brown sugar and ¼ tsp. salt. Sprinkle steak with remaining ¼ tsp. salt. Grill steak, pineapple, and scallions, covered, 3 to 4 minutes on each side or until steak is desired degree of doneness and pineapple and scallions are tender.

3 Let steak stand 5 minutes; cut diagonally across grain into thin slices. Finely chop pineapple and scallions; place in a small bowl, and stir in salsa. Serve steak over rice, and top with pineapple salsa.

Total time:
15 minutes

GRILL THE PINEAPPLE
AND SCALLIONS
WITH THE STEAK!

Total time:
20 minutes

CONVENIENCE
PRODUCTS LIVE UP TO
THEIR NAME HERE.

PEPPER STEAK WITH ROASTED RED PEPPER PESTO

SERVES 4

1¼ beef sirloin steak,
   1½ inches thick (1½ lb.)

3 tsp. coarse ground black
   pepper

½ tsp. table salt

2 Tbsp. olive oil

1 (7-oz.) container refrigerated basil pesto

1 (7-oz.) jar roasted red bell
   peppers, drained and
   chopped

1 Tbsp. lemon juice

1 Sprinkle both sides of steak with pepper and salt; brush with oil. Heat grill pan over medium-high heat until hot. Add steak; cook 10 to 15 minutes, turning once, or to desired degree of doneness. Remove steak from pan to cutting board; let stand 5 minutes.

2 Meanwhile, in small bowl, mix pesto, roasted peppers, and lemon juice. Cut steak against the grain into thin slices. Serve with red pepper pesto.

Simple
Suppers

SNAPPY SIDES

Fresh, colorful veggies, savory sautés, biscuits, and more

CUCUMBER SALAD WITH TOMATOES

The fresh and bright flavors of tomatoes, sweet onions, and cucumbers are wonderful served alongside grilled meats or sandwiches.

 SERVES 8

⅓ cup olive oil

¼ cup red wine vinegar

1 Tbsp. fresh lemon juice

¾ tsp. table salt

½ tsp. black pepper

4 cups grape tomatoes, halved

2½ cups sliced seedless or English cucumber

¼ cup chopped fresh parsley

¼ cup thinly sliced sweet onion

2 Tbsp. chopped fresh oregano

1 Whisk together first 5 ingredients in a large bowl. Add tomatoes and remaining ingredients; toss well.

2 Let stand at least 10 minutes before serving to allow the flavors to infuse.

Snappy Sides

Total time:
20 minutes

**SUBSTITUTE
RED ONIONS
IF YOU LIKE.**

PUB SLAW WITH BEETS

Capers and pickled beets balance salty and sour tastes in this favorite slaw with onions and chopped eggs.

 **SERVES 10**

½ cup mayonnaise

¼ cup dill pickle relish

2 Tbsp. drained capers

1 Tbsp. malt vinegar

1 Tbsp. stone-ground mustard

1 tsp. chopped fresh tarragon

½ tsp. freshly ground pepper

1 (10-oz.) package finely shredded cabbage

½ cup thinly sliced red onion

2 hard-cooked eggs, peeled and chopped

1¼ cups canned sliced pickled beets, cut into thin strips

1 Stir together first 7 ingredients in a large bowl. Add cabbage, onion, and eggs; toss well. Add beets; toss gently just until combined.

Snappy Sides

FENNEL SALAD WITH WATERMELON

Quality honey and fresh lime juice make all the difference when livening up juicy watermelon and fennel. You can also pair this quick dressing with grilled shrimp or chicken.

 SERVES 4-6

3 Tbsp. fresh lime juice

2 Tbsp. olive oil

1 Tbsp. honey

¼ tsp. kosher salt

¼ tsp. freshly ground black pepper

3¼ cups thinly sliced fennel bulb

3 cups cubed watermelon

¼ cup chopped fresh mint

2 oz. (about ½ cup) crumbled feta cheese

1 Combine first 5 ingredients, stirring with a whisk. Combine fennel and watermelon in a large bowl. Drizzle dressing over watermelon mixture; toss gently. Sprinkle with mint and cheese.

Snappy Sides

Total time:
10 minutes

**THIS CAN BE MADE
AHEAD UP TO
4 HOURS.**

Total time:
18 minutes

USE MILD SAUSAGE FOR A MILDER VERSION.

MAQUE CHOUX

Instead of chopping all the vegetables into little pieces, we sliced the bell pepper and okra to give this dish better texture and a more interesting look—but chop if you must!

 SERVES 8

- ¼ lb. spicy smoked sausage, diced
- ½ cup chopped sweet onion
- ½ cup sliced green bell pepper
- 2 garlic cloves, minced
- 3 cups fresh corn kernels
- 1 cup sliced fresh okra
- 1 cup peeled, seeded, and chopped tomato (½ lb.)

1 Sauté sausage in a large skillet over medium-high heat 3 minutes or until browned. Add onion, bell pepper, and garlic, and sauté 5 minutes or until tender.

2 Add corn, okra, and tomato; cook, stirring often, 10 minutes. Season with salt and pepper to taste.

Note: We tested with Conecuh Original Spicy and Hot Smoked Sausage.

GREEK-STYLE GREEN BEANS

 SERVES 4

1 lb. fresh green beans, trimmed

1 Tbsp. olive oil

1 cup grape tomatoes, halved

1 Tbsp. chopped fresh oregano leaves

¼ tsp. table salt

¼ tsp. coarsely ground black pepper

½ cup crumbled feta cheese (2 oz.)

1 In a 4-qt. saucepan, place steamer basket. Add 1 cup water; heat to boiling. Add green beans to basket. Cover; cook 4 to 5 minutes or until crisp-tender.

2 In a 12-inch skillet, heat oil over medium heat. Add green beans, tomatoes, oregano, salt, and pepper. Cook 30 to 60 seconds or just until tomatoes are heated. Sprinkle with cheese.

Add a little crunch and smoky flavor to these beans by topping with 2 Tbsp. each chopped red onion and crumbled bacon.

Snappy Sides

Total time:
15 minutes

FIND WASHED AND TRIMMED BEANS IN PRODUCE SECTION.

Total time:
12 minutes

FOR THE BEST FLAVOR,
STICK TO FRESH—NOT
FROZEN—VEGETABLES.

SQUASH-AND-ONION SAUTÉ

This homestyle side is the perfect addition to a holiday spread or as part of a well-rounded veggie plate.

 SERVES 6-8

- 2 Tbsp. butter
- 2 medium-size yellow squash, sliced into half moons
- 2 medium zucchini, sliced into half moons
- 1 small onion, sliced
- 2 garlic cloves, minced
- 2 tsp. sugar
- ½ tsp. table salt
- ¼ tsp. freshly ground black pepper
- 2 Tbsp. thinly sliced fresh basil

1 Melt butter in a large nonstick skillet over medium heat; add squash, zucchini, onion, and garlic, and sauté 6 to 8 minutes or until vegetables are tender. Stir in sugar, salt, and black pepper; sauté 2 minutes. Remove from heat; sprinkle with basil.

Snappy Sides

ROASTED CARROTS WITH FETA VINAIGRETTE

This salad melds char, spice, and creaminess. The key to roasting veggies is to use similarly sized pieces. Spread them evenly on a baking sheet, and roast in a very hot oven until just tender.

 SERVES 4

- 2 lb. small carrots in assorted colors
- 1 Tbsp. sorghum syrup or honey
- 4 Tbsp. extra virgin olive oil, divided
- 1 tsp. kosher salt
- 1 tsp. ground cumin
- ½ tsp. freshly ground black pepper
- ¼ tsp. dried crushed red pepper
- 1 shallot, minced
- 2 Tbsp. red wine vinegar
- 2 oz. feta cheese, crumbled
- 1 ripe avocado, sliced
- 2 Tbsp. fresh cilantro leaves
- 1 Tbsp. roasted, salted, and shelled pepitas (pumpkin seeds)

1 Preheat oven to 500°. Toss carrots with sorghum and 2 Tbsp. olive oil. Sprinkle with kosher salt and next 3 ingredients; toss to coat. Place carrots in a lightly greased jelly-roll pan. Bake at 500° for 15 to 20 minutes or until tender, stirring halfway through.

2 Stir together shallot and vinegar. Add salt and pepper to taste. Stir in remaining 2 Tbsp. olive oil; stir in feta.

3 Arrange carrots and avocado on a serving platter. Drizzle with vinaigrette. Sprinkle with cilantro and pepitas.

Total time:
20 minutes

**FIND PEPITAS
IN THE NUT AISLE.**

Total time:
20 minutes

HOMEMADE BREAD-CRUMBS ADD SAVORY CRUNCH.

LEMON BROCCOLINI

Although Broccolini looks like young broccoli, it's actually a different plant. It's a hybrid of broccoli with a very similar flavor. Don't confuse it with the look-alikes broccoli rabe or rapini.

 SERVES 4-6

1   cup (½-inch) French bread baguette cubes
2   Tbsp. butter
1   garlic clove, pressed
2   Tbsp. chopped fresh flat-leaf parsley
2   tsp. lemon zest
1½ lb. fresh Broccolini
2   Tbsp. fresh lemon juice
1   Tbsp. olive oil

1 Process bread in a food processor 30 seconds to 1 minute or until coarsely crumbled.

2 Melt butter with garlic in a large skillet over medium heat; add breadcrumbs, and cook, stirring constantly, 2 to 3 minutes or until golden brown. Remove from heat, and stir in parsley and lemon zest.

3 Cook Broccolini in boiling salted water to cover 3 to 4 minutes or until crisp-tender; drain well. Toss Broccolini with lemon juice, olive oil, and salt and freshly ground pepper to taste. Transfer to a serving platter, and sprinkle with breadcrumb mixture.

Snappy Sides

SAUTÉED GARLIC SPINACH

Talk about fast! As soon as the spinach hits the pan, it shrinks in volume dramatically. Add it in two batches if your pan isn't big enough.

 SERVES 4

1   tsp. olive oil
1   garlic clove, pressed
1   (10-oz.) bag fresh spinach

1 Heat olive oil in a nonstick skillet over medium-high heat. Sauté garlic in hot oil 30 seconds. Add fresh spinach to skillet, and cook 2 to 3 minutes or until spinach is wilted. Sprinkle with salt and pepper to taste. Serve spinach with a slotted spoon or tongs.

Turn this side into a steakhouse favorite by stirring in ¼ cup cream cheese and sprinkling with a touch of crushed red pepper.

Snappy Sides

Total time:
5 minutes

**ALL YOU NEED IS
3 INGREDIENTS
AND 5 MINUTES!**

Total time:
20 minutes

TRIM OKRA FIRST
BY CUTTING OFF THE
TIP OF THE STEM.

PAN-FRIED OKRA

This room-temperature side combines hot and crispy fried okra with cool tomatoes and red onion. A squeeze of lime brightens the dish.

 **SERVES 8**

- 2 lb. fresh okra
- ½ cup vegetable oil
- 1 medium-size red onion, thinly sliced
- 2 large tomatoes, seeded and thinly sliced
- 2 Tbsp. lime juice
- 1½ tsp. table salt
- 1½ tsp. black pepper
- 1 tsp. chicken bouillon granules

1 Cut okra in half lengthwise.

2 Pour ¼ cup oil into a large skillet over medium-high heat. Cook okra in hot oil, in batches, 6 minutes or until browned, turning occasionally.

3 Remove from skillet, and drain well on paper towels. Repeat with remaining okra, adding remaining ¼ cup oil as needed. Cool.

4 Stir together onion and next 5 ingredients in a large bowl; add okra, tossing to coat. Serve at room temperature.

HERBED PEAS AND ONIONS

You'll be surprised how a little sautéed onion, lemon zest, and fresh herbs will liven up a bag of frozen peas. This is the perfect side for a comfort food meal alongside some mashed potatoes.

 SERVES 6

- 1 cup sliced onion
- 1 Tbsp. olive oil
- 1 (14.4-oz.) bag frozen sweet peas
- ¼ cup chopped fresh basil or mint
- 1 tsp. lemon zest
- ½ tsp. table salt
- ½ tsp. freshly ground black pepper

Garnish: fresh basil or mint leaves

1 Sauté onion in hot oil in a large skillet over medium-high heat 5 minutes or until tender. Add peas; cook, stirring occasionally, 3 minutes or until peas are thoroughly heated. Remove from heat; stir in basil and next 3 ingredients.

Snappy Sides

Give this side a little more color by substituting 1 bag frozen peas and carrots for the sweet peas. Carrots add a bit of sweetness and will also go perfectly with lemon and fresh herbs.

Total time:
14 minutes

SPEED IT UP
BY USING PRE-
CHOPPED ONION.

Total time:
20 minutes

CHOOSE THIN ASPARAGUS FOR THE MOST TENDER RESULT.

ASPARAGUS WITH GREMOLATA

The gremolata garnish of parsley, garlic, and lemon zest adds a fresh flavor. Gremolata can also be sprinkled onto other dishes.

 **SERVES 4**

- ¼ cup chopped fresh flat-leaf parsley
- 2 cloves garlic
- 2 tsp. grated lemon zest
- 1 lb. fresh asparagus
- 2 Tbsp. unsalted butter, melted
- ¼ tsp. table salt
- ¼ tsp. pepper

1 In a food processor, place parsley and garlic. Cover; process until finely chopped. Transfer mixture to a small bowl; stir in lemon zest. Set aside.

2 Snap off tough ends of asparagus. In a 12-inch skillet, bring 1 inch water (salted, if desired) to a boil. Add asparagus. Return to a boil; reduce heat to medium. Cover; cook 5 to 6 minutes or until crisp-tender. Drain.

3 Arrange asparagus on a serving plate. Drizzle with butter; sprinkle with salt and pepper. Top with gremolata.

Give your vegetables a little added heft and protein by topping them with chopped hard-boiled egg.

HOT-OFF-THE-PRESS GARLIC BREAD

By using a combination of melted butter and olive oil, this French bread gets loads of flavor and crispiness without burning.

 SERVES 8

3   minced garlic cloves
2   Tbsp. olive oil
2   Tbsp. butter, melted
½   tsp. crushed red pepper
1   (16-oz.) loaf French bread
2   Tbsp. chopped chives

1 Preheat oven to 350°. Stir together garlic, olive oil, butter, and crushed red pepper.

2 Cut bread in half. Brush with garlic mixture; bake at 350° for 13 minutes or until golden. Sprinkle with chopped chives.

Turn this loaf into garlicky cheese bread by simply sprinkling with shredded mozzarella or fontina halfway through baking.

Snappy Sides

Total time:
18 minutes

ADD COLD CUTS AND
CHEESE TO MAKE
SANDWICHES.

Total time:
18 minutes

IF BATTER SPLATTERS TOO MUCH, TURN DOWN THE HEAT.

HOT-WATER CORNBREAD

Prepare this cornbread at the last minute so you can serve it piping hot.

 SERVES 6-8

2   cups white cornmeal
¼   tsp. baking powder
1¼   tsp. table salt
1   tsp. sugar
¼   cup half-and-half
1   Tbsp. vegetable oil
1   cup boiling water
Vegetable oil

1 Combine cornmeal and next 3 ingredients in a bowl; stir in half-and-half and 1 Tbsp. oil. Gradually add about 1 cup boiling water, stirring until batter is the consistency of grits.

2 Pour oil to depth of ½ inch into a large heavy skillet; place over medium-high heat. Scoop batter into a ¼-cup measure; drop into hot oil, and fry, in batches, 3 minutes on each side or until golden. Drain well on paper towels. Serve immediately.

1

original recipe

CHEDDAR DROP BISCUITS

 **SERVES 6-8**

2 cups all-purpose baking mix

½ cup (2 oz.) shredded sharp Cheddar cheese

¾ cup milk

Cooking spray

2 Tbsp. butter, melted

½ tsp. dried parsley, crushed

½ tsp. garlic powder

1 Preheat oven to 450°. Combine baking mix and cheese; make a well in center of mixture. Add milk, stirring just until moistened.

2 Drop dough by rounded tablespoonfuls, 2 inches apart, onto a baking sheet coated with cooking spray. Bake at 450° for 8 minutes or until golden.

3 Combine butter, parsley, and garlic powder; brush over warm biscuits.

Total time: **14 minutes**

BRUSH WITH GARLIC BUTTER AND SERVE HOT!

2

PARMESAN CHEESE **+** FRESH PARSLEY AND BASIL **=**

PARMESAN HERB
BISCUITS

Prepare Cheddar Drop Biscuits as directed,
substituting ½ cup grated Parmesan for
Cheddar. Substitute 1 tsp. chopped fresh
parsley and 1 tsp. chopped
fresh basil for the dried parsley.

3

BUTTERMILK **+** BACON **=**

BUTTERMILK BACON
BISCUITS

Prepare Cheddar Drop Biscuits
as directed, substituting buttermilk
for milk. Stir in ½ cup chopped
cooked bacon along with the cheese.

4

JALAPEÑO PEPPER **+** CILANTRO **=**

JALAPEÑO CHEDDAR
BISCUITS

Prepare Cheddar Drop Biscuits as
directed, adding in 1 tsp. minced
jalapeño pepper along with the milk.
Substitute 1 tsp. fresh chopped
cilantro for the dried parsley.

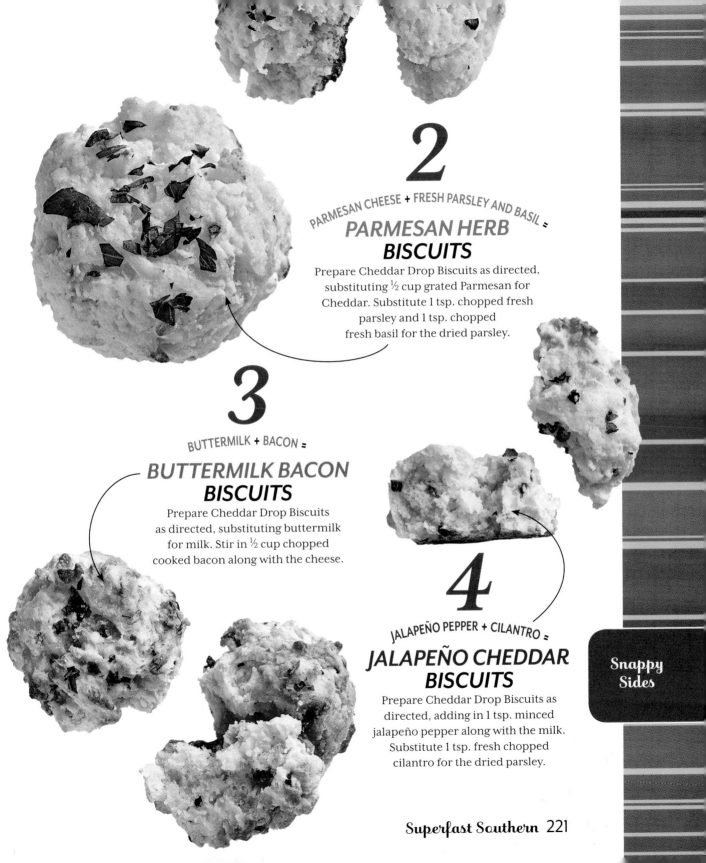

HURRY UP, SUGAR

Sweet and simple treats for when you need dessert fast

Total time:
5 minutes

SCOOP AND POUR FOR THE SIMPLEST DESSERT OF ALL.

FIZZY, FRUITY ICE CREAM FLOATS

A frosty dessert is never this easy. Guests can pick their favorite fruit-flavored soft drink and let the colorful creations flow.

 SERVES 6

4   cups vanilla ice cream

6   (12-oz.) fruit-flavored soft drinks, such as grape, orange, lime, or black cherry

1 Place 2 (⅓-cup) scoops of vanilla ice cream into each of 6 large glasses. Pour soft drinks over ice cream.

Create an ice-cream-float bar by laying out the ice cream and soda choices plus flavored syrups, whipped cream, and colorful straws.

Hurry Up,
Sugar!

TIPSY BERRIES

Here's a summery spin on ambrosia. The berries are easy and elegant to prepare, adding fresh color to any dinner table.

 SERVES 4-6

1   (16-oz.) container fresh strawberries, sliced

1   cup fresh blueberries

½   cup fresh raspberries

¼   cup shaved fresh coconut

2   Tbsp. bourbon

2   tsp. sugar

1 Stir together strawberries, blueberries, raspberries, coconut, bourbon, and sugar; let stand 10 minutes. Serve with a slotted spoon.

Hurry Up, Sugar!

Total time:
15 minutes

**BUY SLICED STRAW-
BERRIES TO MAKE IT
EVEN QUICKER.**

Total time:
15 minutes

**SPRINKLE WITH
ANY KIND OF
CRUMBLED COOKIE.**

BROWN SUGAR PEARS

Cooking the pears in the skillet rather than baking them in the oven makes this recipe come together in a hurry.

 SERVES 4

- 1　Tbsp. lemon juice
- 3　Anjou pears, peeled and quartered
- 3　Tbsp. butter
- ¼　cup firmly packed brown sugar
- 1　tsp. vanilla extract

Crème fraîche or vanilla ice cream

Gingersnaps, crumbled

1 Sprinkle lemon juice over pears; toss.

2 Melt 1 Tbsp. butter in a large nonstick skillet over medium-high heat. Sauté pears 2 minutes or until browned. Add remaining 2 Tbsp. butter and brown sugar to skillet. Reduce heat to medium-low; cook, stirring often, 3 to 4 minutes or until pears are tender. Remove from heat, and stir in vanilla.

3 Serve warm pears and syrup with a dollop of crème fraîche or ice cream. Sprinkle with gingersnap crumbs.

Hurry Up, Sugar!

TRÉS LECHES TRIFLES WITH SUMMER BERRIES

This dessert is a delectable cross between summer pudding and trés leches (three milks) cake.

SERVES 12

- 1 qt. fresh strawberries, quartered
- 1 pt. fresh raspberries
- 1 pt. fresh blackberries
- 1 pt. fresh blueberries
- ½ cup sugar
- 1 (16-oz.) angel food cake
- 1 (14-oz.) can sweetened condensed milk
- ½ cup half-and-half
- 2 cups whipping cream, whipped

1 Combine first 5 ingredients in a large bowl; toss gently.

2 Meanwhile, cut cake into 1-inch cubes. Whisk together condensed milk and half-and-half in a medium bowl.

3 Divide half of cake cubes among 12 (12-oz.) glasses (about 3 to 4 cubes per glass). Top each with 1 Tbsp. milk mixture. Top each with about ¼ cup berry mixture. Divide half of whipped cream among glasses (about ¼ cup each). Repeat layers once.

Hurry Up, Sugar!

Total time:
20 minutes

**MAKE THESE
IN MINI SIZE FOR
A CROWD!**

Total time:
10 minutes

THIS RECIPE IS EASILY DOUBLED OR TRIPLED.

BANANA PUDDING

Just like the diner favorite, these miniaturized banana puddings pack in all the yummy layers you remember, but take only a fraction of the time to make!

 **SERVES 3**

- 9 Tbsp. thawed nondairy whipped topping
- 3 small bananas, sliced
- 1 (3.5-oz.) vanilla pudding cup
- 6 vanilla wafers

1 In each of 3 (5-oz.) glasses, layer 1 Tbsp. thawed nondairy whipped topping, 3 banana slices, 1 Tbsp. vanilla pudding, 3 more banana slices, and 1 vanilla wafer. Repeat. Dollop with 1 Tbsp. thawed nondairy whipped topping.

Hurry Up, Sugar!

GRILLED PINEAPPLE WITH COCONUT SORBET

Grilling isn't just for meat and vegetables anymore! Top grilled pineapple with coconut sorbet or vanilla ice cream.

🥣 SERVES 4

- 1 small pineapple, peeled and cored
- ¼ cup packed dark brown sugar
- 2 Tbsp. dark rum
- Cooking spray
- 1 cup store-bought coconut sorbet
- 2 Tbsp. flaked sweetened coconut, toasted

1 Preheat grill to high (400° to 450°) heat.

2 Cut pineapple into 8 (½-inch-thick) rings; place in a medium bowl. Combine brown sugar and rum; pour over pineapple. Let stand 5 minutes.

3 Place pineapple on grill rack coated with cooking spray. Grill 3 minutes. Turn pineapple over; grill 4 minutes or until caramelized, basting frequently with remaining brown sugar mixture. Place 2 pineapple slices on each of 4 plates; top each with ¼ cup coconut sorbet and 1½ tsp. toasted coconut. Serve immediately.

Hurry Up, Sugar!

Total time:
15 minutes

USE PRESLICED PINEAPPLE FROM THE PRODUCE SECTION.

1

original recipe
PINEAPPLE PARFAITS

SERVES 4

- 1½ cups diced fresh pineapple
- 2 Tbsp. light brown sugar
- 1 Tbsp. olive oil
- ¼ tsp. vanilla extract
- 4 cups low-fat Greek yogurt
- 4 Tbsp. chopped salted pistachios

1 Sauté pineapple and brown sugar in hot olive oil in a skillet over medium-high heat 2 to 3 minutes or until lightly browned. Remove from heat; stir in vanilla.

2 Spoon 1 cup yogurt into each of 4 bowls, and top with one-fourth of pineapple mixture and 1 Tbsp. pistachios.

Total time:
15 minutes

BELIEVE IT OR NOT, IT'S GOOD FOR YOU, TOO!

2

STRAWBERRIES + WALNUTS + BALSAMIC GLAZE =

BALSAMIC
STRAWBERRY
PARFAITS

Prepare Pineapple Parfaits as directed,
substituting halved fresh strawberries for
pineapple and toasted chopped walnuts for
pistachios. Top each parfait with a drizzle
of balsamic glaze.

3

CARAMELIZED
PINEAPPLE SMOOTHIES

Prepare Pineapple Parfaits through step 1.
Place pineapple pieces and syrup in a blender
with yogurt. Blend until smooth. Pour into
glasses, and top with pistachios.

4

PEACHES + SLICED ALMONDS =

FRESH PEACH
PARFAITS

Prepare Pineapple Parfaits as
directed, substituting fresh peach slices
for pineapple and sliced almonds
for pistachios.

*Hurry Up,
Sugar!*

FREE-FORM STRAWBERRY CHEESECAKE

Powdered sugar saves time and dissolves instantly when stirred into berries for an almost effortless dessert.

 SERVES 6

- 2 cups fresh strawberries, sliced
- 4 Tbsp. powdered sugar, divided
- 1½ cups ready-to-eat cheesecake filling
- 1 tsp. lime zest
- 1 Tbsp. lime juice
- 6 crisp gourmet cookies, crumbled

Garnishes: crisp gourmet cookies, lime slices

1 Stir together strawberries and 2 Tbsp. powdered sugar.

2 Stir together cheesecake filling, lime zest, lime juice, and remaining 2 Tbsp. powdered sugar.

3 Spoon cheesecake mixture into 6 (6-oz.) glasses or ramekins. Sprinkle with crumbled cookies. Top with strawberries. Serve immediately.

Note: We tested with Philadelphia Ready-To-Eat Cheesecake Filling and Biscoff cookies.

Hurry Up, Sugar!

Total time:
20 minutes

**SWAP THE SPRING-
FORM PAN FOR
CHEESECAKE CUPS.**

Total time:
20 minutes

ROOM-TEMPERATURE LIMES ARE THE EASIEST TO JUICE.

KEY LIME PIE

Prepare this pie in a flash ahead of time and just let it cool completely before serving. You can make it up to one day ahead; keep chilled.

SERVES 8

1   (14-oz.) can fat-free sweetened condensed milk
¾   cup egg substitute
2   tsp. Key lime zest (about 2 limes)
½   cup fresh Key lime juice
1   (6-oz.) reduced-fat ready-made graham cracker piecrust
1   (8-oz.) container fat-free whipped topping, thawed

Garnishes: lime twists

1 Preheat oven to 350°.

2 Process first 4 ingredients in a blender until smooth. Pour mixture into piecrust.

3 Bake at 350° for 10 to 12 minutes or until golden. Cool completely on a wire rack (about 1 hour), and top with whipped topping.

Hurry Up, Sugar!

BLUEBERRY COBBLER WITH SUGARED STAR SHORTCAKES

Look for sparkling sugar at craft stores. In a pinch, granulated sugar is a good substitute.

 SERVES 10

- 2 pt. fresh blueberries
- ½ cup granulated sugar
- 1 Tbsp. lemon juice
- ⅛ tsp. almond extract
- 2 (12-oz.) cans refrigerated buttermilk biscuits
- 1 Tbsp. coarse sparkling sugar

Sweetened whipped cream

1 Preheat oven to 400°. Combine first 4 ingredients in a medium sauce-pan. Cook over medium-high heat 5 minutes or until bubbly and sugar dissolves. Remove from heat.

2 Separate biscuits, and flatten each into a 3½-inch circle. Cut with a 3-inch star-shaped cutter, and place on a lightly greased baking sheet; sprinkle with sparkling sugar, press-ing to adhere. Bake at 400° for 8 min-utes or until lightly browned.

3 Spoon blueberry mixture into 10 bowls; top with biscuits. Serve with whipped cream.

Note: We tested with Pillsbury Grands! Jr. Golden Layers Buttermilk Biscuits.

Hurry Up, Sugar!

Total time:
15 minutes

IT'S AN OH-SO-SIMPLE
USE FOR REFRIGER-
ATED BISCUITS.

Total time:
15 minutes

**PHYLLO SHELLS THAW
IN JUST 5 MINUTES!**

CARAMEL-CHOCOLATE TARTLETS

Dulce de leche is the star in these bite-size treats. Look for it in the baking aisle or in the international foods section.

 SERVES 30

- 2 (1.9-oz.) packages frozen mini phyllo shells (30 shells), thawed
- 1 (13.4-oz.) can dulce de leche (caramelized sweetened condensed milk)
- 1 cup semisweet chocolate morsels
- ⅓ cup salted dry-roasted peanuts, chopped

1 Place phyllo shells on a baking sheet. Spoon 1 heaping tsp. dulce de leche into each shell. In small microwave-safe bowl, microwave chocolate morsels uncovered at HIGH about 1 minute, stirring once, until smooth. Spoon 1 tsp. melted chocolate over dulce de leche in each shell.

2 Sprinkle tartlets with peanuts. Freeze 1 minute to set chocolate. Store, covered, in refrigerator.

Hurry Up, Sugar!

Total time:
15 minutes

A 3-INGREDIENT DESSERT YOU COULD MAKE EVERY NIGHT!

BISCUIT BEIGNETS

Some call them "Bonuts" (biscuits + doughnuts), but we just call them divinely delicious! No one will guess these doughnuts started as canned biscuits.

 SERVES 6

1   (12-oz.) can refrigerated
    buttermilk biscuits

Vegetable Oil

Powdered sugar

1 Separate biscuits into individual rounds, and cut into quarters. Pour oil to a depth of 2 inches in a Dutch oven, and heat over medium heat to 350°. Fry, in batches, 1 to 1½ minutes on each side or until golden. Drain on paper towels; dust with powdered sugar.

Hurry Up, Sugar!

DEEP-FRIED MOONPIES

These little treats are so decadent and rich, you'll want to cut into fourths before serving!

 SERVES 8

1½ cups all-purpose flour

1 cup milk

2 large eggs

1 Tbsp. sugar

⅛ tsp. table salt

4 MoonPies

2 cups panko (Japanese breadcrumbs)

Vegetable oil

1 Whisk together first 5 ingredients in a medium bowl. Dip MoonPies in batter until coated; dredge in panko.

2 Pour oil to depth of 2 inches into a Dutch oven; heat over medium heat to 350°. Fry MoonPies, in batches, 20 to 30 seconds on each side or until golden brown. Drain on a wire rack over paper towels. Cut into quarters to serve.

Hurry Up, Sugar!

Total time:
10 minutes

IF A CUBE OF BREAD
SIZZLES IN IT, THE OIL'S
HOT ENOUGH.

METRIC EQUIVALENTS

The information in the following charts is provided to help cooks outside the United States successfully use the recipes in this book. All equivalents are approximate.

EQUIVALENTS FOR DIFFERENT TYPES OF INGREDIENTS

Standard Cup	Fine Powder	Grain	Granular	Liquid Solids	Liquid
	(ex. flour)	(ex. rice)	(ex. sugar)	(ex. butter)	(ex. milk)
1	140 g	150 g	190 g	200 g	240 ml
¾	105 g	113 g	143 g	150 g	180 ml
⅔	93 g	100 g	125 g	133 g	160 ml
½	70 g	75 g	95 g	100 g	120 ml
⅓	47 g	50 g	63 g	67 g	80 ml
¼	35 g	38 g	48 g	50 g	60 ml
⅛	18 g	19 g	24 g	25 g	30 ml

LIQUID INGREDIENTS BY VOLUME

¼ tsp	=						1 ml
½ tsp	=						2 ml
1 tsp	=						5 ml
3 tsp	=	1 Tbsp	=		½ fl oz	=	15 ml
		2 Tbsp	=	⅛ cup	1 fl oz	=	30 ml
		4 Tbsp	=	¼ cup	2 fl oz	=	60 ml
		5⅓ Tbsp	=	⅓ cup	3 fl oz	=	80 ml
		8 Tbsp	=	½ cup	4 fl oz	=	120 ml
		10⅔ Tbsp	=	⅔ cup	5 fl oz	=	160 ml
		12 Tbsp	=	¾ cup	6 fl oz	=	180 ml
		16 Tbsp	=	1 cup	8 fl oz	=	240 ml
		1 pt	=	2 cups	16 fl oz	=	480 ml
		1 qt	=	4 cups	32 fl oz	=	960 ml
					33 fl oz	=	1000 ml = 1 l

LENGTH

(To convert inches to centimeters, multiply the number of inches by 2.5.)

1 in =			2.5 cm	
6 in =	½ ft =		15 cm	
12 in =	1 ft =		30 cm	
36 in =	3 ft =	1 yd =	90 cm	
40 in =			100 cm	= 1 m

COOKING/OVEN TEMPERATURES

	Fahrenheit	Celsius	Gas Mark
Freeze Water	32° F	0° C	
Room Temperature	68° F	20° C	
Boil Water	212° F	100° C	
Bake	325° F	160° C	3
	350° F	180° C	4
	375° F	190° C	5
	400° F	200° C	6
	425° F	220° C	7
	450° F	230° C	8
Broil			Grill

DRY INGREDIENTS BY WEIGHT

(To convert ounces to grams, multiply the number of ounces by 30.)

1 oz =	¹⁄₁₆ lb =	30 g
4 oz =	¼ lb =	120 g
8 oz =	½ lb =	240 g
12 oz =	¾ lb =	360 g
16 oz =	1 lb =	480 g

Index

ISBN-13: 978-0-8487-4352-9
ISBN-10: 0-8487-4352-0
Library of Congress Control Number: 2014939741
Printed in the United States of America
First Printing 2014

OXMOOR HOUSE

Editorial Director: Leah McLaughlin
Creative Director: Felicity Keane
Art Director: Christopher Rhoads
Executive Food Director: Grace Parisi
Senior Editor: Rebecca Brennan
Managing Editor: Elizabeth Tyler Austin
Assistant Managing Editor: Jeanne de Lathouder

SUPERFAST SOUTHERN

Editor: Allison E. Cox
Senior Designer: J. Shay McNamee
Assistant Test Kitchen Manager: Alyson Moreland Haynes
Recipe Developers and Testers: Tamara Goldis, R.D.;
   Stefanie Maloney; Callie Nash; Karen Rankin;
   Wendy Treadwell, R.D.; Leah Van Deren
Food Stylists: Victoria E. Cox, Margaret Monroe Dickey,
   Catherine Crowell Steele
Photography Director: Jim Bathie
Senior Photographer: Hélène Dujardin
Senior Photo Stylists: Kay E. Clarke, Mindi Shapiro Levine
Senior Production Manager: Sue Chodakiewicz
Assistant Production Manager: Diane Rose Keener

CONTRIBUTORS

Project Editor: Melissa Brown
Compositors: Amy Bickell, Frances Higginbotham
Copy Editors: Julie Bosche, Adrienne Davis
Indexer: *Marra*thon Production Services
Fellows: Ali Carruba, Kylie Dazzo, Elizabeth Laseter,
   Anna Ramia, Deanna Sakal, April Smitherman,
   Megan Thompson, Tonya West, Amanda Widis
Food Stylist: Charlotte Autry
Photographer: Johnny Autry
Photo Stylist: Charlotte Autry

***SOUTHERN LIVING*®**

Editor: Sid Evans
Creative Director: Robert Perino
Managing Editor: Candace Higginbotham
Executive Editors: Hunter Lewis, Jessica S. Thuston
Deputy Food Director: Whitney Wright
Test Kitchen Director: Robby Melvin
Test Kitchen Specialist/Food Styling:
   Vanessa McNeil Rocchio
Test Kitchen Professional: Pam Lolley
Recipe Editor: JoAnn Weatherly
Style Director: Heather Chadduck Hillegas
Director of Photography: Jeanne Dozier Clayton
Photographers: Robbie Caponetto, Laurey W. Glenn,
   Hector Sanchez
Assistant Photo Editor: Kate Phillips Robertson
Photo Coordinator: Chris Ellenbogen
Senior Photo Stylist: Buffy Hargett Miller
Assistant Photo Stylist: Caroline M. Cunningham
Photo Administrative Assistant: Courtney Authement
Editorial Assistant: Pat York

TIME HOME ENTERTAINMENT IN

President and Publisher: Jim C
Vice President and Associate P
Vice President, Finance: Vanda
Executive Director, Marketing
Publishing Director: Megan Pe
Assistant General Counsel: Sin